Buddhist Buildings

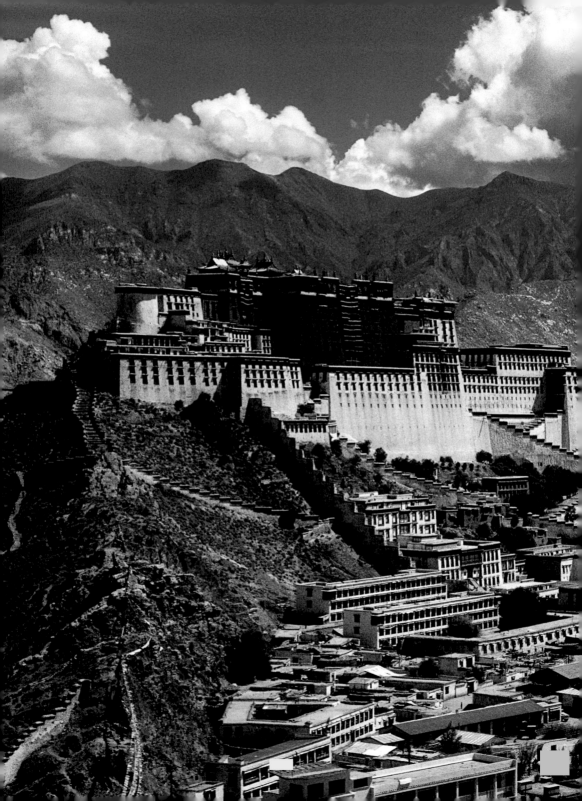

General View of Potala Palace, Lhasa, Tibet
preceding page

In the 15th year of the reign of Zhenguan (641), Emperor Taizong of the Tang Dynasty, Songzan Gampu had a palace built for Princess Wencheng on the Red Mountain. Buddhist followers compared it to Putuo Mountain, the residence of Guanyin Bodhisattva, and in Tibetan it is called "Potala". Continuous warfare resulted in the palace of this Turphan Empire mostly being burned down. In the 2nd year of the reign of Shunzhi (1645), Emperor Shizu of the Qing Dynasty, Dalai V rebuilt the palace on the site of Potala Palace and it took eight years to complete the construction of the White Palace, which he established as his residence. From this time onwards, the Dalai Lamas all regarded Potala Palace as their residence, from there to rule over the whole of Tibet. The Red Palace and its western veranda were gradually added later, the former to house the soul pagoda of the Dalai Lama, the latter to provide living quarters for the monks, both giving the palace the grand scale characterizing it today.

The Excellence of Ancient Chinese Architecture

BUDDHIST BUILDINGS

Buddhist Monasteries, Pagodas and Stone Caves

Wei Ran

China Architecture & Building Press

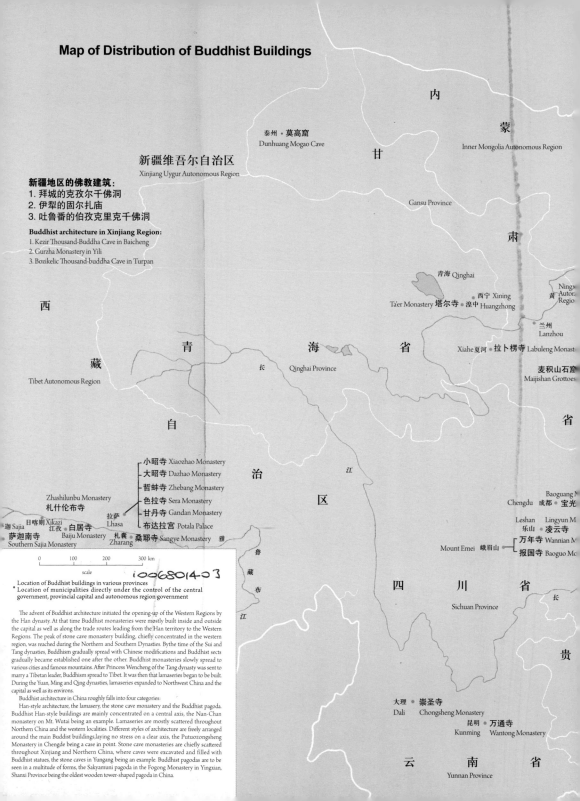

Map of Distribution of Buddhist Buildings

泰州 · 莫高窟
Dunhuang Mogao Cave

内 蒙
Inner Mongolia Autonomous Region

甘
肃

Gansu Province

新疆维吾尔自治区
Xinjiang Uygur Autonomous Region

新疆地区的佛教建筑：
1. 拜城的克孜尔千佛洞
2. 伊犁的固尔扎庙
3. 吐鲁番的伯孜克里克千佛洞

Buddhist architecture in Xinjiang Region:
1. Kezir Thousand-Buddha Cave in Baicheng
2. Gurzha Monastery in Yili
3. Bozikelic Thousand-buddha Cave in Turpan

青海 Qinghai

西
藏

Ta'er Monastery 塔尔寺

西宁 Xining
湟中 Huangzhong

Ning
Autor.
Regio

黄

兰州
Lanzhou

青 海 省

Qinghai Province

Xiahe 夏河 拉卜楞寺 Labuleng Monast

麦积山石窟
Maijishan Grottoes

Tibet Autonomous Region

长

自

治

区

江

省

小昭寺 Xiaozhao Monastery
大昭寺 Dazhao Monastery
哲蚌寺 Zhebang Monastery
色拉寺 Sera Monastery
甘丹寺 Gandan Monastery
布达拉宫 Potala Palace

Zhashilunbu Monastery
札什伦布寺
日喀则 Xikazi
江孜
迦 Sajia
萨迦南寺
Southern Sajia Monastery

拉萨
Lhasa
白居寺
Baiju Monastery

札囊
Zharang

桑耶寺
Sangye Monastery

雅

鲁
藏
布
江

Baoguang
Chengdu 成都 宝光
Leshan Lingyun M
乐山 凌云
万年寺 Wannian
Mount Emei 峨眉山
报国寺 Baoguo M

四 川 省

Sichuan Province

贵

州

长

0   100   200   300 km
scale   ┆0068014-03
• Location of Buddhist buildings in various provinces
• Location of municipalities directly under the control of the central
government, provincial capital and autonomous region government

The advent of Buddhist architecture initiated the opening-up of the Western Regions by
the Han dynasty. At that time Buddhist monasteries were mostly built inside and outside
the capital as well as along the trade routes leading from the Han territory to the Western
Regions. The peak of stone cave monastery building, chiefly concentrated in the western
region, was reached during the Northern and Southern Dynasties. Bythe time of the Sui and
Tang dynasties, Buddhism gradually spread with Chinese modifications and Buddhist sects
gradually became established one after the other. Buddhist monasteries slowly spread to
various cities and famous mountains. After Princess Wencheng of the Tang dynasty was sent to
marry a Tibetan leader, Buddhism spread to Tibet. It was then that lamaseries began to be built.
During the Yuan, Ming and Qing dynasties, lamaseries expanded to Northwest China and the
capital as well as its environs.

Buddhist architecture in China roughly falls into four categories:
Han-style architecture, the lamasery, the stone cave monastery and the Buddhist pagoda.
Buddhist Han-style buildings are mainly concentrated on a central axis, the Nan-Chan
monastery on Mt. Wutai being an example. Lamaseries are mostly scattered throughout
Northern China and the western localities. Different styles of architecture are freely arranged
around the main Buddist buildings,laying no stress on a clear axis, the Putuozongsheng
Monastery in Chengde being a case in point. Stone cave monasteries are chiefly scattered
throughout Xinjiang and Northern China, where caves were excavated and filled with
Buddhist statues, the stone caves in Yungang being an example. Buddhist pagodas are to be
seen in a multitude of forms, the Sakyamuni pagoda in the Fogong Monastery in Yingxian,
Shanxi Province being the oldest wooden tower-shaped pagoda in China.

大理 · 崇圣寺
Dali   Chongsheng Monastery

昆明 万通寺
Kunming   Wantong Monastery

云 南 省

Yunnan Province

吉林省
Jilin Province

区

自 治

河
Hebei Province

辽
Liaoning Province

省

沈阳 Shenyang

Fengguo Monastery
Yixian 义县 奉国寺
Qianshan 千山 龙泉寺 Longquan Monastery

Chengde
承德

河

Hanging Monastery
悬空寺
Huayan Monastery 上华岩寺
Huayan Monastery 下华岩寺
Yungang Monastery 云冈石窟

慈灯寺
呼和浩特 Chleng Monastery
Huhhot 大同 浑源
Datong Hunyuan

佛宫寺 应县
Fogong Monastery Yingxian
五台山
Wutai Mountain

显通寺 Xiantong Monastery
塔院寺 Tayuan Monastery
南禅寺 Nan-Chan Monastery
佛光寺 Foguang Monastery
碧山寺 Bishan Monastery
镇海寺 Zhenhai Monastery

北京 Beijing

天津 Tianjin

渤 海
Bouhai Sea

溥仁寺 Puren Monastery
溥善寺 Pushan Monastery
普乐寺 Pule Monastery
安远庙 Anyuan Temple
广缘寺 Guangyuan Monastery
普佑寺 Puyou Monastery
普宁寺 Puning Monastery
广安寺 GuangAn Monastery
殊像寺 Shuxiang Monastery
罗汉堂 Hall of Arhat
普陀宗乘之庙 Putuozongsheng Monastery
须弥福寿之庙 Xumifushou Monastery

陕

山

太原 永祚寺 正定
Yongzuo Monastery

西

省

西

汾

隆兴寺 Longxing Monastery
广惠寺 Guanghui Monastery
法源寺 Fayuan Monastery

千佛山兴国寺
Xingguo Monastery on
Qianfo Mountain

山

独乐寺 Dule Monastery
观音寺 Guanyin Monastery

黄

Hongtong 河
洪洞
广胜上寺
Upper Guangsheng Monastery

北响堂山中窟
Middle Cave in Northern Xiangtangshan
邯郸 Handan

东

济南
Jinan

省

Shandong Province

运

潭柘寺 Tanzhe Temple
碧云寺 Biyun Monastery
卧佛寺 Sleeping Buddha Monastery
雍和宫 Lama Temple
广济寺 Guangji Monastery
智化寺 Zhihua Monastery
真觉寺 Zhenjue Monastery
法源寺 Fayuan Monastery
大正觉寺 Greater Zhengjue Monastery

Monastery
gfu Monastery
ng Monastery 西

Xian
西安

长安 Chang'an
净业寺 Jinye Monastery
终南山 Zhongnanshan

河

省

Luoyang
洛阳

黄

Kaifeng
开封

白马寺 Baima Monastery
永宁寺 Yongning Monastery
龙门石窟 Longmen Monastery

Dengfeng
登封

少林寺 Shaolin Monastery
嵩岳寺 Songyue Monastery

Futu Monastery
浮图寺
徐州
Xuzhou

江
苏
Jiangsu Province

省

Yellow Sea

海

Xiangji Monastery
Monastery
Monastery

湖

北

省

Hubei Province

水

河

南

Henan Province

安

Anhui Province

省

合肥
Hefei

Nanjing
南京

河

苏州
Suzhou

Shanghai
上海市

龙华寺
Longhua Monastery

Ganlu Monastery
Zhiyuan Monastery
Huacheng Monastery

甘露寺
祇园寺
化城寺

杭州
Hangzhou

普陀山
Mount Putuo

当阳 玉泉寺
Dangyang Yuquan Monastery

Echeng 鄂城 西山古灵泉寺
Gulingquan Monastery in the Western Hills

Mount Jiuhua 九华山

Mount Tiantai
天台山 国清寺
Guoqing Monastery

Puji Monastery
普济寺 Puji Monastery
慧济寺 Huji Monastery
不肯去观音院
Unwilling-to-leave
Guanyin Monastery

Jiujiang 九江 能仁寺 Nengren Monastery
Mount Lu 庐山 东林寺
Donglin Monastery

浙

江

hou Province
省
Guiyang
fu Monastery on
ing Mountain

Nanchang 南昌 佑民寺
Youmin Monastery

麓山寺 长沙 Changsha
Lushan Monastery

南台寺 衡山 Hengshan
Nantai Monastery

湖

南

Hunan Province

江

西

Jiangxi Province

省

Zhejiang Province

福

建

省

Fujian Province

福州
Fuzhou

寒山寺 Hanshan Monastery
云岩寺 Yunyan Monastery
戒幢寺 Jiechuang Monastery

灵谷寺 Linggu Monastery
栖霞寺 Qixia Monastery

台

湾

省

台北
Tai-pei

开元寺 泉州
Kaiyuan Monastery Quanzhou

台
湾
海
峡

台
湾

西壮族自治区
Guangxi Region

广

东

省

Guangdong Province

Guangzhou
广州 海幢寺 Haichuang Monastery

Taiwan Province

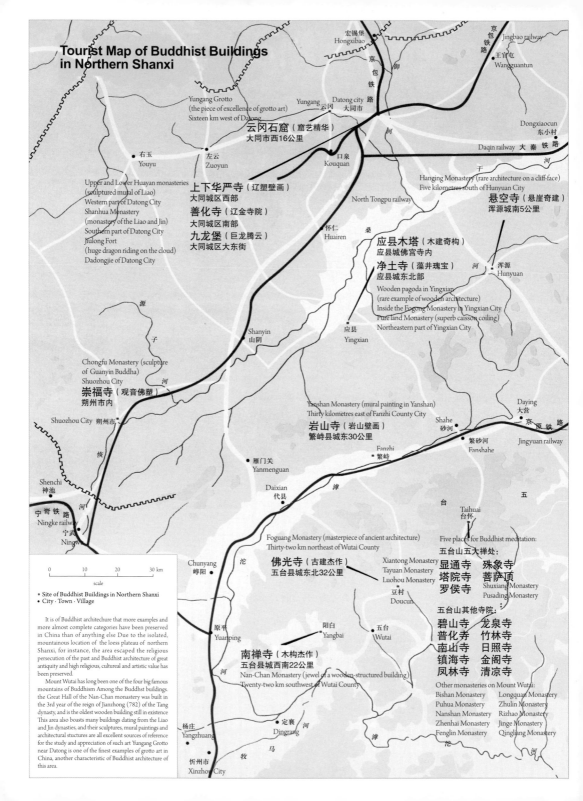

Tourist Map of Buddhist Buildings in Northern Shanxi

宏锡堡
Hongxibao

京包铁路 Jingbao railway

王官屯
Wangguantun

右玉
Youyu

左云
Zuoyun

Yungang Grotto
(the piece of excellence of grotto art)
Sixteen km west of Datong

云冈
Yungang

大同市
Datong city

东小村
Dongxiaocun

云冈石窟（窟艺精华）
大同市西16公里

Daqin railway 大秦铁路

口泉
Kouquan

干
河

Upper and Lower Huayan monasteries
(sculptured mural of Liao)
Western part of Datong City
Shanhua Monastery
(monastery of the Liao and Jin)
Southern part of Datong City
Julong Fort
(huge dragon riding on the cloud)
Dadongjie of Datong City

North Tongpu railway

Hanging Monastery (rare architecture on a cliff-face)
Five kilometres south of Hunyuan City

上下华严寺（辽塑壁画）
大同城区西部

善化寺（辽金寺院）
大同城区南部

九龙堡（巨龙腾云）
大同城区大东街

怀仁
Huairen

桑

悬空寺（悬崖奇建）
浑源城南5公里

应县木塔（木建奇构）
应县城佛宫寺内

净土寺（藻井瑰宝）
应县城东北部

Wooden pagoda in Yingxian
(rare example of wooden architecture)
Inside the Fogong Monastery in Yingxian City
Pure land Monastery (superb caisson coiling)
Northeastern part of Yingxian City

浑源
Hunyuan

河

源
子

山阴
Shanyin

Shanyin

应县
Yingxian

Chongfu Monastery (sculpture
of Guanyin Buddha)
Shuozhou City

崇福寺（观音佛塑）
朔州市内

Shuozhou City 朔州市

恢

Yanshan Monastery (mural painting in Yanshan)
Thirty kilometres east of Fanzhi County City

大营
Daying

砂河
Shahe

京原铁路 Jingyuan railway

岩山寺（岩山壁画）
繁峙县城东30公里

繁砂河
Fanshahe

繁峙
Fanzhi

Fanzhi

Jingyuan railway

Shenchi
神池

河

雁门关
Yanmenguan

代县
Daixian

淳

台
五

宁岢铁路
Ningke railway

宁武
Ningwu

台怀
Taihuai

Foguang Monastery (masterpiece of ancient architecture)
Thirty-two km northeast of Wutai County

Five places for Buddhist meditation:

五台山五大禅处：

莼阳
Chunyang

佛光寺（古建杰作）
五台县城东北32公里

Xiantong Monastery
Tayuan Monastery
Luohou Monastery

显通寺 **殊象寺**
塔院寺 **菩萨顶**
罗侯寺

Shuxiang Monastery
Pusading Monastery

豆村
Doucun

五台山其他寺院：

原平
Yuanping

阳白
Yangbai

五台
Wutai

碧山寺 **龙泉寺**
普化寺 **竹林寺**
南山寺 **日照寺**
镇海寺 **金阁寺**
凤林寺 **清凉寺**

河

南禅寺（木构杰作）
五台县城西南22公里

Nan-Chan Monastery (jewel of a wooden-structured building)
Twenty-two km southwest of Wutai County

Other monasteries on Mount Wutai:

Bishan Monastery   Longquan Monastery
Puhua Monastery   Zhulin Monastery
Nanshan Monastery   Rizhao Monastery
Zhenhai Monastery   Jinge Monastery
Fenglin Monastery   Qingliang Monastery

杨庄
Yangzhuang

定襄
Dingrang

河

牧

马

忻州市
Xinzhou City

scale

0   10   20   30 km

* Site of Buddhist Buildings in Northern Shanxi
• City · Town · Village

It is of Buddhist architechure that more examples and
more almost complete categories have been preserved
in China than of anything else Due to the isolated,
mountainous location of the loess plateau of northern
Shanxi, for instance, the area escaped the religious
persecution of the past and Buddhist architecture of great
antiquity and high religious, cultureal and artistic value has
been preserved.

Mount Wutai has long been one of the four big famous
mountains of Buddhism Among the Buddhst buildings.
the Great Hall of the Nan-Chan monastery was built in
the 3rd year of the reign of Jianzhong (782) of the Tang
dynasty, and is the oldest wooden building still in existence
This area also boasts many buildings dating from the Liao
and Jin dynasties, and their sculptures, mural paintings and
architectural stuctures are all excellent sources of reference
for the study and appreciation of such art Yungang Grotto
near Datong is one of the finest examples of grotto art in
China, another characteristic of Buddhist architecture of
this area.

宏锡堡
Hongxibao

京包铁路
Jingbao railway

Contents

General Introduction

Notes on the Photographs

North China

Central China

West China

Appendices

Editor's Note

- The series consists of ten volumes, each of which deals with respectively palace architecture, imperial mausoleums, imperial gardens, private gardens, vernacular dwellings, Buddhist buildings, Taoist buildings, Islamic buildings, ritual and ceremonious buildings and defense structures..

- Each volume is basically composed of four sections, i.e. general introduction, colour photographs, glossary and chronology of major events.

- The general introduction describes the background, development process, architectural characteristics of different types of buildings and is complimented with photographs and drawings.

- The colour photographs are arranged in the order of building distribution area or the time when the building was completed. The series contains about 1,700 exquisite colour photographs, which are attached with captions explaining the location, construction time, and artistic and technical features.

- Each volume is accompanied with layout plan, drawing of recovered buildings, distribution map and travel guide to mark the location of famous buildings and cultural attractions in the vicinity.

- The glossary is arrayed according to the sequence of strokes of Chinese characters, which is a reference for general readers.

- Chronology of major events is affiliated with each volume of the series. Chinese traditional chronology is adopted in the annals of the series, and is also indicated in the Christian era for easy reference.

Preface 1

China enjoys a long and profound history of ancient architecture. Her verifiable artifacts could be dated back to 7,000 years ago from Hemudu ruins in Yuyao to Banpo ruins in Xi'an. Of course, architecture underwent a long process from primitiveness to sophistication before the Warring States, while in the Qin and Han dynasties, it gained an apparent progress along with the development of production and unification of the country. Moreover, in over a thousand years of the prosperous Tang Dynasty to the Ming and Qing dynasties, it reached several unprecedented peaks which were embodied by diversified building forms and refined planning and exquisite construction.

The love of architecture is the love of history and culture. China Architecture & Building Press (CABP), from the very beginning of its founding, has defined the sorting out and publication of traditional Chinese architecture and the enhancement of Chinese culture as one of important themes in its mission. In 1950s and 1960s, many monographs on the subject by experts such as Liang Sicheng, Liu Dunzhen, Tong Jun, Liu Zhiping and others were published. In early 1980s when China was just opened to the outside world, CABP set aside a special fund for publication of academic books on ancient Chinese architecture despite of the limited financial capability then. As a result, large academic albums of Ancient *Chinese Architecture, Ancient Architecture in Chengde, the Art of Chinese Gardens, the Buildings of Confucius Temple in Qufu, Ancient Buildings of Putuoshan, Summer Palace as well as* five volumes of *History of Ancient Chinese Architecture* were put forth continuously. Those books have proved to be of high academic and practical values in consolidation, conservation and protection of the national treasure.

The Excellence of Ancient Chinese Architecture in English is a series of ten volumes on various aspects of the ancient Chinese architecture, which offer a comprehensive coverage of the art, highlighted by the supreme quality of the photos as well as plenty of drawings of plans, sections and perspectives. The easy description would lead to a comprehension of the cultural essence of Chinese architecture, and appreciation of the aesthetics and philosophy embodied by the art. The authors are famous Chinese experts who have long been engaged in the study of the related subjects, whose dedication makes the series authoritative and informative for interested laymen and specialists alike. Now the Excellence of Ancient Chinese Architecture is published. It is a happy event. I believe that it will serve as a door for all those who are interested in the study of ancient Chinese architecture.

Zhou Yi | Former President
China Architecture & Building Press

Former Chairman, Committee on Publication of Science Books
Vice Chairman, Chinese Association of Publishers

Preface 2

As history advances in the new era of the 21st century, China is once again becoming the focus of worldwide attention. The rich variety of her landscape, the wisdom of her people, the current unprecedented economic growth, and the wealth of her cultural heritage are all becoming the subject of worldwide interest.

In China's extensive and profound cultural treasury, ancient architecture is one of the important components, which, in a sense, is of a symbolic nature. The beauty and elegance of ancient Chinese architecture has a uniqueness of its own in the world architectural system. The strict formality of the city layouts, the lively arrangement of village settlements, the grouping of buildings around courtyards, the comprehensive building code for wood structures, the great variety of colour and architectural form, the perfect harmony of the decorative and structural functions of building elements, the integration of furniture, interior decoration, painting, sculpture and calligraphy into a comprehensive art of architecture, all go to manifest the distinctive characteristics of the traditional Chinese culture. A perusal of the country's magnificent palaces and temples, her tranquil and intricate gardens, the wide variety of her vernacular dwellings, and the exquisiteness of her pavilions and roofed walkways, will lead to a better understanding of China and her people. When one comes to study China's ancient architecture, he will have a deeper comprehension of the oriental philosophy of the "oneness of nature and man" inherent in the architectural forms, as well as of the Chinese people's respect for Confucianism, the expression of their philosophical meditation on time and space through material forms, and their all-embracing aesthetic tastes.

Now the *Excellence of Ancient Chinese Architecture* is published. I believe the vivid and colourful photos will render our readers an enjoyment of aesthetics, and the easy descriptions will facilitate our readers in understanding the cultural essence of ancient Chinese architecture. Under the trend of globalization, it will surely promote the academic exchange internationally and deepen the cultural cooperation among different peoples of the world.

Ye Rutang | Former Vice Minister
Ministry of Construction

The Excellence of Ancient Chinese Architecture

————

Buddhist Buildings

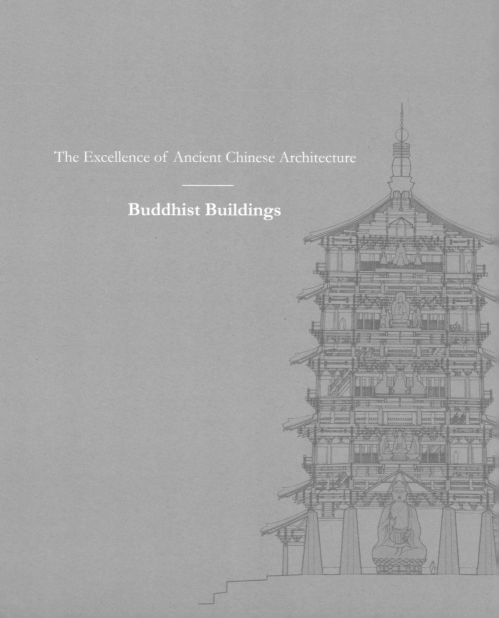

General Introduction

The Formation and Development of Chinese Buddhism

—— Explaining Buddhism by Mysticism and Supplementing Mysticism with Buddhism

Journeying through the vast expanses of China, with its towering mountains, wide rivers, deep and secluded valleys and its bustling cities and towns, one often comes across Shaman Buddhist temples, their doors open to greet the faithful and visited by hundreds of inquisitive travellers. The large Buddhist monasteries have attracted great numbers of pilgrims for a thousand years; others take

Fengxian Monastery in the Longmen Grottoes

The biggest in scale of those in the Longmen grottoes of the Tang Dynasty, the Fengxian monastery was completed in the 2nd year of the reign of Shangyuan (675), Emperor Gaozong of the Tang Dynasty. The principal statue is the Lusshena Buddha sitting cross-legged in meditation. The whole statue is 17.14 m high; its head 4 m tall and the two ears 1.9 m long. It wears a Kasaya shawl and its face is well filled out and handsome, its two eyes peaceful and reserved and the corners of the mouth upturned in a smile. A magnificent statue, the expression conveyed is one of solemnity, wisdom, far-sightedness and kindness: in spirit infinitely compassionate and merciful. On its left and right are two docile and pious disciples, two solemn and reserved Bodhisattvas, the powerful and mighty Heavenly King and guards staring angrily, their brows knitted. The composition and the quality of the sculpture are perfect.

the form of small temples and solitary nunneries found looking out over the boundless ocean, nestling on plains or low-lying land surrounded by mountain ranges or situated further up on mountain slopes.

It is, however, not only the beauty of their setting that makes Buddhist monasteries so impressive, but the strength of their unique wooden-structured architecture. This ancient form of building, part of China's rich cultural heritage, has fortunately been preserved in a great number of these Buddhist buildings, and studying them gives not only an insight into how they developed historically but also how a unique Chinese culture of its own came into being.

Chinese traditional thinking that lays stress on solving the practical problems of human life and religious thought on the afterlife had, since ancient times, been neglected. Though Taoism believed in supernatural beings and possessed a strong religious flavour, its main theory was devoted to teaching people how to preserve their health. As to the problems of the soul, it had no satisfactory explanation. This vacuum was filled by a new religion imported from abroad, namely Buddhism.

I. The Initial Spread of Buddhism

From about the 6th to the 5th century B.C, equivalent to the Spring and Autumn Period in China, there was in ancient India a small country named Capilore lying at the foot of the Himalayas. Travelling one day through the countryside, Prince Siddhartha saw just how bitter life was for so many people. This set him thinking, and he decided to become a monk, in the hope that through asceticism he would find a way of relieving people of their suffering. After years of self-denial and search for enlightenment he finally attained Buddhahood and founded a primitive theory of Buddhism .

After the establishment of Buddhism, Chaodama Siddhartha was honoured as Sakyamuni meaning sage of the "Sakya" tribe.

The essential ideas of the belief held in esteem by Sakyamuni can be summed up as: 1. Life is full of sorrow and bitterness. 2. This sorrow and bitterness originate from desire. 3. Sorrow can only be relieved by the state of "Nirvana." 4. Only through the practice of Buddhism and following the "eight right ways," can one be freed from the bitterness of samsara (transmigration) and reach the faramita of Nirvana.

The 300 years after Sakyamuni's death saw his theories spreading throughout India due to repeated recitation and extensive preaching by his disciples. By the 3rd century A.D., thanks to the energetic support of the 3rd king Ashoka, of the Maurya Empire, Buddhism had began to spread beyond the confines of India, to Myanmar and Sri Lanka in the south, to central and western Asia in the north and to China in the east. It was eventually to become a religion of worldwide influence.

Buddhism was first founded in India. Before spreading to China, it spread northward into Parthia and the countries of the Western Regions. It then spread into China. At the time Indian Buddhism had started to be disseminated, the Chinese Emperor Wudi of the Han Dynasty twice sent Zhang Qian on a diplomatic mission aimed at contacting the Western Regions and gaining their support for a policy of joint resistance to the Huns. A channel was thus opened between China and the countries of central and western Asia, and it was along this road that not only officials, special envoys and merchants of the western Han Dynasty travelled, but also monks, taking with them Buddhist scriptures into China.

As to the exact date Buddhism spread into China, the legends vary, due to the fact that historical records were unclear. In addition, when Buddhism first spread into China, it was not particularly attractive to society in general, and, more importantly, was not taken notice of by those in authority. People still did not understand the difference between this foreign Buddhism and the Yellow Emperor, Laotse, Confucianism and Taoism with which they were familiar.

As already mentioned, there was much confusion as to just when Buddhism spread into China, but it came to be accepted that it was in the 10th year of Yongping of the Eastern Han Dynasty's reign (67A.D.), when, as the more detailed historical documents relate, Emperor Mingdi, having dreamt that a golden man had appeared before him in the night, sent an envoy to seek the Buddhist dharma. In the same year, the Indian monks, Niemoteng and Zhufalan, brought Buddhist scriptures and an image of Buddha to China, settled in Luoyang in Henan Province, and set about translating the earliest, and still extant, Chinese book of scripture (The Forty-Two Chapter Scriptures), which, at the time, played an important role in the spread and development of Buddhism in China.

The translation of Buddhist scripture was, in the early years, the basic means of dissemination. People had to be convinced that this completely new foreign form of belief could be universally acknowledged by society. To make things easier, Confucian and Taoist terms were used to explain Buddhist scripture and theory. As the practice of Buddhist ceremonies such as lecture-giving and the expounding of Buddhist teachings was not developed at this stage, there was no need for Buddhist temples to be built on a great scale. Apart from guest houses for the monks and buildings used for work of scripture translation, no traditional Indian monasteries were built, nor was there any embryonic form of a Chinese Buddhist monastery.

II. The Beginnings and the Translation of Scripture

The end of the Eastern Han Dynasty (25-220) to the Wei (220-265), Jin (256-420) and the Northern and Southern dynasties (420-589) represented an important period in the history of Buddhist development in China. Besides introducing and translating Buddhist scriptures on a large scale, Buddhist ceremonies such as giving lectures and expounding Buddhist teachings were further developed. Over a period of nearly 400 years, such outstanding Buddhist figures as An Shi Gao, Zhiloujachen, Fotudeng, Dao An, Hui Yuan, Jiumoloshi and others successfully introduced Buddhism into China by their remarkable preaching. The translations and commentaries of these great masters, well-versed in both Sanskrit and Chinese, were not only easy to understand but also possessed considerable literary merit, and were thus enjoyed by both the common people and those of higher ranking as well as by the royal family and the imperial kinsmen .

An Shi Gao, crown prince of Parthia, visited many countries in the Western Regions and was well-versed in several languages. During the 20 years from the 2nd year of the reign of Jianhe (148 A.D.) of Emperor Hengdi of the Han Dynasty to the 4th year of the reign of Jianing of Emperor Lingdi of the Han Dynasty, he translated over 30 volumes of Buddhist scriptures, mostly devoted to the study of the Chan-Sect of Hynayana Buddhism. He paid special attention to using the "numeral method" and tried to classify the numerous concepts in Buddhist scripture by numerals, such as "four essentials", "eight right ways", "twelve causes", "five implications" and "eighteen circles", thus simplifying the whole for beginners.

Zhiloujachen of the Indo-Scyths, a contempoary of An Shi Gao translated a scripture book on Mahayana Buddhism. This had a great influence on the development of Chinese Buddhism and Chinese ideology. Another scripture book translated by him expounded the Mahayana Buddhist outlook and openly declared Amitabha's Western Pure Land concept .

Up to the time of Wei (220-265) and Jin (265-420), mysticism was in vogue. Some Buddhist scholars explained the emptiness of Prajna (the highest wisdom) by mysticism in order to further the Buddhist cause, and Buddhist terms were explained by using Chinese philosophical ones. Mysticism was thus used to explain Buddhism, Buddhism used to supplement mysticism in order to gain more people's acceptance of what was a foreign religion. As a result, the "six schools of thought and seven religious sects" came into being. Steps were being taken for the modification of Buddhism to suit Chinese requirements.

Another important figure in Chinese Buddhist history was Dao An of the Eastern Jin Dynasty (317-420). He made a great and important contribution to the dissemination of Buddhism in China. First, he translated, sorted out and wrote a large number of scripture books, collected a list of Buddhist scriptures that had been translated and wrote a preface to them. He also compiled a "Collection of Scriptures." Secondly, he drew up ceremonies and standards for monks and nuns, set up the first Sangha system in China and abolished all monks' and nuns' original surnames, replacing them by 'Sakya'. This played a great role in strengthening Buddhist monastic regulations. Thirdly, he devoted himself to giving publicity to dharma and preaching Buddhism, establishing the largest Buddhist organization of the time. Disciples following him as master numbered thousands. These disciples, having mastered their studies, dispersed in all directions, spreading Buddhist dharma. Among them, the most famous was Huiyuan, who later became the religious leader of the Eastern Jin Dynasty (317-420), and founder of the Pure Land Sect.

The earliest translations of Buddhist scriptures in China were the result of individual activities that were scattered and unsystematic. The organized and large-scale translation of Buddhist scripture books was undertaken by Jiumolosh in the early years of the 5th century. In 401 A.D., Yao Xing, the monarch of the Later Qin, invited Jiumolosh to Chang'an, to take charge of scripture translation. Under the aegis of the monarch, a huge scripture translation centre for Buddhist rites came into being under the guidance of Jiumolosh, employing nearly 5,000 Buddhist monks. Jiumolsh stayed at Chang'an for more than ten years and translated altogether 35 categories of Buddhist scriptures, commandments and theories of the Mahayana and Hynayana School, totaling 294 volumes. These translated Buddhist scriptures provided the Zhongguan Sect established by Longshu with systematic explanations and commandments. Jiumolosh initially translated the original ideas into Chinese, but, in the case of those parts not suited to a literal translation from the Sanskrit into the Chinese, he sought to adapt the one to the other, searching for the original meaning, making bold additions and deletions. His works were not only gratefully received by the Buddhist monks of the Central Plains but also had an influence on the development of the Buddhist literature of later generations.

By the time of the Wei, Jin and Northern and Southern dynasties, Buddhist scriptures had basically been translated. This enabled further establishment of religious sects and a rebellion against the original religion to take place. More attention was given, as far as translation was concerned, to a more Chinese-oriented approach. Buddhist followers increased unprecedentedly and Buddhism in China was beginning to reach its first high peak.

Thanks to Buddhism's widespread popularity in both government and public circles, as well as the frequency of Buddhist ceremonies and scripture translations, Buddhist temples began to be built in China on a large scale during this period.

Tradition has it that during the Western Jin (265-317) period, there were altogether 180 monasteries in the eastern and western capitals (Luoyang and Chang'an) and monastery pictures were worshipped in the capital. The building of Buddhist temples in the Eastern Jin (317-420) became even more widespread. Well-known monasteries such as Donglin Temple, Daochang Temple, Waguan Temple, Chang'an Temple were all built in this period. With Donglin Temple as centre, the great Master Huiyuan, founder of the Pure Land Sect, preached Buddhist dharma, making it known far and wide. The famous painter Gu Kaizhi painted his mural painting in Waguan Temple, "*A Temple under the Sun.*" A few of the big monasteries like Dunhuang, Yungang, Longmen, Maiji, Bingling also began to be built during this period.

Buddhism was twice wiped out in the north of China during the reigns of Emperor Taiwu (557-581) of the Northern Wei (386-534) and Emperor Wudi of the Northern Zhou (557-581), with a period of 130 years in-between. In the south, however, the new religion grew from strength to strength, and by the reign of Emperor Wudi of Liang (502-557), was flourishing. The emperor himself was a devout Buddhist believer, well-versed in the essence of Confucianism, Taoism and Buddhism. According to the "*Southern History*", Emperor Wudi of Liang had several times sacrificed himself to save the Tongtai Monastery. Thanks to his active advocacy, in Jiankang over 500 Buddhist temples were built alone; Da' aijing, Zhidu, Guangzhai, Jietuo, Kaishan and other temples being examples. The poet Du Mu of the Tang Dynasty wrote the following lines, "Of the four hundred-and-eighty monasteries of the Southern Dynasty, how many towers and terraces loom in the mystic rain?", lines which are still enjoyed today. During the four historical periods of the Song, Qi, Liang and Chen of the Southern Dynasty (420-479), over 8,000 temples were built, with 180,000 Buddhist monks and nuns in residence. Among these temples, the

Tongtai Monastery was once described as follows, "Towers and pavilions, hall and terraces, houses and corridors gorgeously decorated, soaring to the sky nine-grade high; paired appearance, everlasting serene by "*Volume 11, Records of Three Treasures in Past Dynasties*".

During the Northern Dynasty (386-534), not only were many cave temples built, but the architecture of temples and pagodas also made large advances. Among these buildings, the most famous was the Yongning Monastery pagoda built by the Queen Mother Ling, who lived during the reign of Emperor Xiaoming of the Northern Wei (386-534). In China there were many famous painters, among them two specializing in the drawing of Buddhist figures. One was Cao Zhongda of the Northern Qi (550-571), the other Wu Daozi of the Tang Dynasty (618-907). Their representation of Buddha differed, in that the former gave him a close-fitting robe, the latter, a wide-fitting one with a loose-fitting belt that seemed to float in the air; hence the sayings, 'Wu dai cao yi' (Wu's belt and Cao's clothing) or 'Cao yi chu shui' (Cao's clothing just appearing above the water) and 'Wu dai dang feng' (Wu's belt floating in the air). Both painters continued to enjoy fame throughout later generations.

III. The Establishment and Prosperity of the Buddhist Sects

After Indian Buddhism was introduced into China, a considerable amount of Buddhist scripture was translated. During the process of translation, Indian Buddhism gradually merged with Chinese traditional culture, and after constant digestion and absorption, as well as devoted study and the bringing forth of new ideas by eminent monks over several generations, Buddhism with unique Chinese characteristics finally came into being. The Sui (581-618) and Tang (618-907) dynasties were when Chinese Buddhism reached its zenith.

Many independent theoretic systems of religious sects arose, a fact that can be taken to indicate the establishment of Buddhism in China or that Buddhism had became completely integrated into the Chinese culture. The Buddhist sects established during the Sui and Tang dynasties were: the San-lun Sect (three-theories sect), the Pure Land Sect, Tiantai Sect, the Buddhist Image Sect, the Commandment Sect, the Chen Sect, the Huayan Sect and the Tantra Sect, eight major religious sects.

San Lun Sect: This religious sect was established on the theoretic basis of the Mid-theory, the Twelve Categories Theory and the Hundred Theory

Pagoda in the Xiangji Monastery

The Xiangji monastery was the ancestral hall of the Pure Land Sect, no longer in existence. Only the pagoda in the Xiangji monastery still stands high at the confluence of the Yu and Li rivers. It was built in the 2nd year of Shenlong (706) of the Tang Dynasty in memory of Master Shandao. The original pagoda had 13 storeys, but only 10 now remain. It is a tower pagoda with close eaves. Square railings were added to the four corners of the building. Red in colour, it is a fine and dexterous construction.

translated by Jiumolosh. Its founder was an Indian monk of the 3rd century. It was established after the eminent monk Jizang, who lived during the reign of Sui Emperor Yangdi, had voiced criticism of all schools of thought prevalent during the Wei, Jin and Northern and Southern dynasties. It was, however, after Jizang, soon replaced by the Tiantai Sect, which was close in its teaching to the realities of the Han territory. The sect was later introduced into Japan by the Japanese monk Chi Taka and others, who established a branch sect during the time of Nara. The Qixia Monastery in Nanjing is the ancestral hall of the San Lun Sect.

The Pure Land Sect: A religious sect that emphasizes the Western Paradise of Amitabha. In the Eastern Jin Dynasty (317-420), the well-known Buddhist monk Huiyuan, standing in front of the Amitabha image of Lushan Mountain, formed an association which pledged to go to the Western Pure Land. Up to the reign of the Tang Emperor Gaozong, the great master Shan Dao guided the fortunes of the Pure Land Sect for 30 years, writing, painting, teaching and organizing. This sect became highly popular with simple folk as its teachings were easy to follow; a believer being able to attain final enlightenment and reach the Land of Ultimate Blessing by devotedly calling upon Buddha Amitabha.

The Pure Land Sect has the Xiangji Monastery in Chang'an County of Shaanxi Province as its ancestral hall.

The Tiantai Sect: With Fahua Sutra as its basis and Dazhi Dulun (Buddhist theory of Bodhisattva Longshu) as its guiding force, the Tiantai Sect blends all aspects of Buddhist thinking and Chinese traditional Confucianism, forming at the time a new sect with unique Chinese characteristics. The fourth ancestor Zhiyi is taken as its real initiator. He put forward wu shi ba jiao to expound the essence of the scriptures and advocated yi xin san guan (one mind and three concepts) as the visual concept for the practice of Buddhism, producing the Buddhist Mahayana concept unique to China. Because Zhiyi lived over a long period in the Guoqing Monastery of Tiantai Mountain in Zhejiang Province, later generations came to regard it as the ancestral hall of the Tiantai Sect. In 900 A.D., the Japanese monk Mo Kiyo arrived in China. He learned and mastered the religious doctrine of the Tiantai Sect . Returning to Japan, he established the Japan Lotus Sect there.

The Buddha Image Sect: This religious sect supports the yoga-based set of beliefs practised by Mahayana Buddhism in India, expounding and propagating the argument of the Buddha image and Wei Shi (knowledge). Hence, it was also known as the Weishi Sect. The founder of the Buddha Image Sect, Xuan Zang, journeyed to India to seek dharma. After a long and solitary journey full of hardship, he returned to Chang'an after 17 years, bringing with him over 650 Buddhist scripture books. Supported by Emperor Taizong of the Tang Dynasty, he spent the next 19 years translating scripture at the Hongfu and Greater Ci'en monasteries, thus laying the foundation for the theoretic basis of the Buddha Image Sect . After Xuan Zang died, his disciples wrote many scholarly works and went on expanding the former's teaching. Among them, the most successful was Kuiji. Because both Xuan Zang and Kuiji lived for a long time at the Greater Ci'en (Grace) Monastery, the Buddha Image Sect was also called the Ci'en Sect and the monastery became its ancestral hall.

The Commandment Sect: A religious sect devoted to the unified Commandment of Buddhism. During the Cao and Wei period of the Three Kingdoms (220-280), Buddhist disciplines and ceremonies celebrating the initiation into monkhood spread to Han territory. Up to the time of the Northern and Southern Dynasties, religious disciplines from outside China were mostly translated into Chinese. Of these, the most influential was "*the four-subdivision Commandment*" of the "*Commandment of Sound-hearing Vehicle.*" Dao

Xuan, a Buddhist monk from Zhongnan Mountain during the Tang Dynasty used the Mahayana creed to explain "*the four-subdivision Commandment*" and changed Hynayana vehicle creed into the Mahayana creed, thus establishing the Nanshan Commandment Sect. The Jingye Monastery on Mt.Zhongnan in Shaanxi Province was accepted (by later generations) as the ancestral hall of the Commandment Sect . During the reign of Kaiyuan of the Tang Dynasty, the Buddhist monk Jianzhen travelled east by sea taking the religious creed to Japan.

The Chan Sect: The founder of this sect was Bodhidarma. When propagated to the 5th ancestor, Hong Ren, it divided into two sects with the Huineng Sect in the south and the Shenxiu Sect in the north. Later, the southern sect gradually became the orthodox school of the Chan Sect whose tenets are: not expounding one's ideas in writing; passing on the belief from a master to a single disciple; that the natural disposition is pure; Buddhist nature is innate; nature as a means of attaining truth and thus enlightenment. During its development, the Chan Sect divided into five schools of thought and seven sects. Among them, Lin Ji and Cao Dong lasted the longest. As the Chan Sect was the product of the successful transformation of foreign Buddhism by Chinese traditional thinking and its native culture, it proved to be the most vital of all Buddhist sects so that in the thousand years that followed, it became a synonym of Chinese Buddhism. The Chan Sect takes the Shaolin Monastery in Henan Province as its ancestral hall, where Bodhidharma used to sit facing the wall in meditation.

The Huayan Sect: Its founder Fa Zang was a Buddhist monk in the Tang Dynasty. Using the concept of being flexible and smooth (Yuan Rong) from the Huayan scriptures as its basis, it called itself the "yuan" religion and put the emphasis on being "flexible and smooth" or "mixing together without hindrance." This philosophy, regarded as the highest state of knowledge, held that all things are without contradiction, and its believers applied it to the reconciliation of various Buddhist sects with the Confucian and Taoist schools of thought. Fa Zang was granted the title of "Xianshou Master" after he had lectured on Huayan scripture to the Tang empress Wu Zetian, and for this reason the sect was also called the Xianshou Sect. It takes the Huayan Monastery on Shaolingyuan, south of Chang'an in Shaanxi Province as its ancestral hall. In the 12th year of the reign of Heavenly Peace (740) in Japan, Shenxiang, an elderly Korean Buddhist monk, established the Japanese Huayan Sect in the Eastern Great Monastery in Nara, Japan.

Temple Gate of the Guoqing Monastery

Located in Zhejiang Province, the Guoqing monastery is the birthplace of the Buddhist Taintai sect. In front of the temple gate with its red wall and black tiles, there is a flat terrace, below which is a stone-paved path flanked by an enclosing wall. The atmosphere is peaceful and secluded, made all the more so by the towering pines, great camphor trees and green bamboo.

The Tantra Sect: This sect practised the Yugo tantric religion, popular in India. During the reign of Kaiyuan (713-741) of the Tang Dynasty, Indian Buddhist monks Shanwuwei, Jingangzhi and Bukong came to China in succession, preaching this religion. With the "Great Sun Sutra" and the "Diamond Sutra" representing its original version, this sect practised three forms of tantra: chanting incantation; gesturing with hands; looking at Buddha in the mind's eye. Later, thanks to the energetic propagation of Bukong, it became a religious sect that practised dharma. The methods practised by this religious sect were very different from the habitual method of thinking in Han territory, and thus it did not last for long. On spreading to Tibet, it blended with the local Ben religion becoming the Diamond Vehicle Tantra Religion becoming widespread all over Tibet. The Daxingshan Monastery in Chang'an, where the Great Master Bukong frequently stayed, became the ancestral hall of this sect.

The establishment of these eight religious sects is a manifestation of how Buddhism infiltrated into China and how it developed. It was a long, slow and careful process, ending ultimately in the amalgamation of Buddhism and traditional Chinese ways of thinking.

The Sui and Tang represented a glorious era of Chinese Buddhism although it was gradually to decline in Han territory during the Song (960-1279) and Ming (1368-1644) dynasties when neo-Confucianism flourished. During the reign of Kaibo (968-975), Emperor Taizu of the Song Dynasty, however, the large-scale production of engravings and paintings "The Tribitaka" (The Complete Collection of Buddhist Sutras) commenced and continued during the Song, Yuan, Ming and Qing dynasties, covering scripture, the commandments and theory, and produced in Chinese, Tibetan, Manchurian, Mongolian and many other languages. The only scripture version existing today is the "Dragon Sutra", inscribed during the reign of Emperor Qianlong of the Qing.

Following the establishment of religious sects during the Sui and Tang dynasties, Buddhism spread, reaching a wider range and social stratum through its preachers using more flexible methods. Each religious sect not only continued

Dayan Pagoda of the Cien (grace) Monastery

South of Xi'an, the Dayan (wild goose) Pagoda had only five storeys with a height of 18 zhang (about 59.4 m) when it was first built. Later, it was rebuilt and repaired several times. During the Ming Dynasty, it received a layer of brick all round, thus being given its present shape. The pagoda now stands at 64 m and the sides of its square base measure 25 m. The seven storeys taper upwards, each with railings at the four corners.

Temple Gate Screen Wall of the Guoqing Monastery

The Guoqing Monastery was first built in the 18th year of the reign of Kaihuang (598) of the Sui Dynasty. Its original name was Tiantai. The existing architecture was mostly completely modified in the 12th year of the Qing Dynasty's Yongzheng (1734). "Ancient monastery of the Sui Dynasty" was engraved on the screen wall outside the temple gate, and at the entrance, an antithetical couplet was engraved on a hanging tablet : "This ancient monastery was first built during the Sui Dynasty,and flourished during the three Tangs, spreading religion far and wide" and "Famous mountain known abroad, resting on five peaks and looking out over two ravines; a famous historical site anew forever."

Temple Gate of Shaolin Monastery

The temple gate of the Shaolin Monastery is 3 bays wide and 6 bays deep. The horizontal board, "Shaolin Monastery ," was written by Emperor Shengzu of the Qing Dynasty. Below the flight of steps on both sides of the tomb passage was a pair of stone lions squatting on an elevated stone base engraved with a lotus pattern. In front of the gate on the east and west sides are two stone archways built during the reign of Jiaqing of the Ming Dynasty.

to adapt its theories to suit prevailing Chinese circumstances, but also set up its own economic and administrative system within the monasteries, using its own ancestral hall as a centre for study, teaching and research. In its ability to absorb many of the beliefs innate to the Chinese, such as respect for one's elders, Buddhism came to be a religion that society in general could accept, and its temples became centres of worship for all classes. People would come to burn joss sticks and make vows, the local authorities and emperors often used the temples for ritual ceremonies and the offering of sacrifices to ancestors. In the *"Six Rituals of Tang"* compiled during the reign of Emperor Xuanzong of the Tang Dynasty, we find the following, "On the anniversary of an ancestor's death celebrated by the state, it is decided that two alms be given at the big temples of the two capitals...... All civil and military officials above the 5th grade and upright

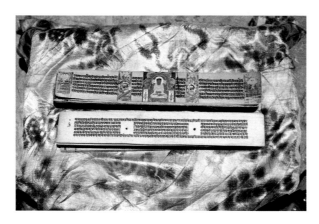

Pattra-Leaf Scripture in Potala Palace

In ancient India, Buddhists wrote Buddhist scriptures on Pattra leaves. After special treatment, they were cut into long and narrow strips and then written on in Sanskrit from left to right. When the piled-up leaves reached the appropriate thickness, they were pressed with wooden boards from both sides, thus forming a complete copy.

officials above the 7th grade should come, offer joss sticks and then retreat. If prefectures outside the capital decide to give alms at each temple and nunnery, officials from the prefecture and county should offer joss sticks. In this case, 81 prefectures should give alms."

Their popularity with the common people, the support of the local authorities and their independent economic position meant that monasteries increasingly prospered.

After Emperor Yangdi of the Sui Dynasty unified the north, he immediately adopted Buddhism using it as one of the tools to strengthen his rule. He not only ordered the reconstruction of the monasteries destroyed by Emperor Wudi of the Northern Zhou Dynasty during his drive against Buddhism, but also ordered the common people to donate money for the writing of scriptures and the production of Buddhist statues. With his energetic support, over 3,700 temples were built and more than 23,000 followers took their vows and became monks. The Eastern Chan Monastery built by Emperor Wudi "has seven storeys, soaring high up into the sky. Its halls stand tall and erect. Its houses are deep and magnificent." (*Stories of Eminent Monks continued, Volume 10.*) By the time of Emperor Xuanzong of Tang, the number of monasteries had increased to 5,300. During the reign of Huichang (841-846), Tang Emperor Wuzong, when Buddhists were persecuted, 260,000 monks resumed secular life and 44,600 monasteries were destroyed. For instance, the Nanchan Monastery south of Lijiazhuang Village in Wutai County of Shanxi Province survived only because of its desolate location. The main hall of this small temple was built over 1,200 years ago, and is the oldest extant wooden structure building.

IV. Tibetan Buddhism (Lamaism)

In the early years of 700 A.D., the 300-year period of sporadic warfare that had gone on before the Tang Dynasty was brought to an end and a strong and powerful political power established. At the same time, on the Qinghai-Tibet Plateau, known as the roof of the world, a young Zampu — Songzan Gampu, succeeded his father Langrilunzan, and took up his cause. He went on expeditions in all directions, expanding his territory and, in the end, unified the long-divided Qinghai-Tibet Plateau, formally declaring the establishment of the Turpan royal court. Before Songzan Gampu, there had been no unified written language. In 500 A.D., Buddhism spread into Tibet, but because of the lack of a written language, there was no way of translating the scriptures, and as a result, Buddhism had difficulty in establishing itself.

1. The Early Stages of Expansion

After Songzan Gampu arrived in Tibet as its ruler, he sent sons of the noble Tunmi Sangbuja and others to Tianzhu (ancient India) and the Western Regions to learn Sanskrit, grammar and the classics on ancient meanings of words from

Dazhao Monastery

Located in the centre of old Lhasa city, the Dazhao Monastery was first built in 647. A monument, inscribed in Chinese and Tibetan and bearing the words, "Monument to the memory of the meeting between uncle and nephew of the Tang and Tubo" stands in front of it. The outer wall of the building is of thick stone painted white, and set in it are ladder windows. Reddish-brown surrounds add a decorative effect. Glistening in the sunlight, the building is set off all the more by the blueness of the sky and the pure white of the clouds.

the Brahman Li Jing, Larebaisenge. Finishing their studies, they returned to Tibet and devised a Tibetan written language. Now that the written language had been unified, Tibet began to have the Buddhist scriptures translated.

From 634-641 A. D., Songzan Gampu got married in succession to Princess Bhrikuti of Nepal and Princess Wencheng of the Tang Dynasty. When the two princesses entered Tibet, they brought with them a huge number of Buddhist scriptures and Buddhist images. This had a great and lasting influence and Buddhism quickly spread. The two princesses had the Dazhao and Xiaozhao monasteries built in Lhasa. Songzan Gampu also built 12 small temples and many places for practising Buddhist rites. The image of Buddhist Guanyin brought into Tibet by Princess Bhrikuti and the image of Sakyamuni brought

to Tibet by Princess Wencheng are still today enshrined and worshipped respectively in Potala Palace and the Dazhao.

The Buddhist scriptures introduced into Tibet in the early years were both exoteric and tantric, influencing chiefly the royal families, as the population in general was still under the influence of the Ben religion. For the few generations of Zampu following Songzan Gampu, life was spent quelling internal revolts and going on expeditions abroad so that they had no time to attend to the development of Buddhism. Things thus came to a standstill.

In the 8th century A. D., during the era of Chisong Dezan, Lianhuasheng, the great Indian master of tantric religion came to Tibet, preaching successfully and increasing the influence of Buddhism in Tibet over the prevailing Ben religion. In

Zong Khaba Statue in the Zhebang
Monastery

The Zhebang Monastery in Gengpei Wuzi in the
western suburb of Lhasa enshrines the statue of
Zong Khaba, founder of the Gelu Sect (Yellow Sect).
His hands overlap, his eyes are half-closed, and a
beaming smile spreads over his face.

The Sakyamuni Buddhist Statue in the
Dazhao Monastery

Brought to Tibet by Princess Wencheng, the statue,
located in Sakyamuni Hall exactly on the axis of
the Juekang main hall, is the Monastery's most
important statue. The 12 gold lamps in front are
reputed to be an original relic.

766 A.D. the Sangye Monastery, the first of its kind, was built in Zharang.

The 9th century, however, saw the large-scale eradication of Buddhism by the Tibetan king, Langdama and supporters of the Ben religion. Many monasteries were destroyed, monks forced to return to secular life, scriptures and statues destroyed. For over a period of 130 years, Buddhism in Tibet was silenced.

2. The Later Stages of Expansion

In the last years of the 10th century A.D., Buddhism gradually spread back to Tibet from Xikang, marking the beginning of the later stage of expansion.

It was a time of greater interflow between Tibetan and Indian Buddhism.

Picture of Dalai V meeting Gush Khan in the Dazhao Monastery / Upper

At the entrance to the eastern wall of the Thousand-Buddhas Corridor in Dazhao Monastery is a picture of Dalai V meeting Kush Khan. The mural, painted in 1648, is a realistic portrayal of the historic meeting to discuss how their enemy Yutuhan could be killed.

Spiritual Pagoda in the Zhebang Monastery / Lower

Inlaid with gold, silver, pearls and jewels, this spiritual pagoda is a fine example of the art of inlaying.

Its initial stage coincided with the time when the Indian Polo Empire was practising a highly tantric religion, especially the Yugo religion. For this reason, a Buddhist tantric religion now enjoyed popularity in Tibet. The 11th century A.D., however, saw Tibetan Buddhism being torn apart by differences of opinion between the followers of a tantric approach and those favouring an exoteric one. At this time, the Banfali Buddhist monk, Adixia, came to Weizang. He devoted himself to preaching Buddhism for 17 years. He translated many scripture books and established the system whereby Tibetan Buddhism practised both tantra and exotericism, but with the former having the upper hand. He also drew attention to how the ceremonies were to be performed.

After Adixia, through long-term expansion and preaching by disciples of various generations, different religious sects came into being. Each of the religious sects laid special emphasis on their own theories and preaching methods. They finally developed a school of their own, entitled "Tibetan Tantra Sect."

The founder of the Gelu Sect of Tibetan Buddhism, Zong Khaba, played an extremely important role in the history of Tibetan Buddhism. Synthesizing the exoteric and tantric religious creed of the various religious sects in Tibet and using the Gedang

Sect as the theoretic basis, he energetically advocated strict adherence to the religious creed and called on the Buddhist monks to reside in the monastery on a permanent basis. He initiated preaching meetings in Lhasa, chose Gandan Monastery as the centre of reform and established the Gelu Sect. Because Zong Khaba advocated wearing a peach-shaped yellow cap, the Gelu Sect was also given the name "Yellow Religion", becoming a highly influential religious movement within Tibetan Buddhism, and influential still today. The thousand years following the stage of later expansion witnessed the gradual development of Tibetan Buddhism into a patriarchal political and religious system. In this it has differed from other sects in the interior. As far as its religious leaders were concerned, the problem of succession was solved by the unique system of reincarnation of the living Buddha, which gradually evolved into a system of the two big living Buddhas of Dalai and Panchen especially after the establishment of the Gelu Sect by Zong Khaba. In the 17th century A.D., supported by Gush

Gandan Pozhang of the Zhebang Monastery

Built by the 2nd generation of Dalai, it was regarded as the palace of the 3rd, 4th and 5th generation of Dalai. The palace has four storeys, the upper two with dwellings for the Dalai, a guest house and a place for Buddhist ceremonies. The front wall surrounding the palace has a two-storeyed veranda running round it.

The Sela Monastery

In the monastery there are Jieba, Maiba, and Abha, three Zhacangs, as well as one Living Buddha's government office. In between them are many Kangcun villages providing residence for the lamas and forming a large-scale architectural complex. The largest building in the monastery is Cuoqin Great Hall used as the meeting place for the whole monastery.

Khan, Shuotebu ruler of Mongolia, Dalai Lama V, Lhosang Jiatso, defeated the forces of other religious sects and entered Lhasa, establishing his rule there. During the 9th year of the reign of Emperor Shunzhi (1652) of the Qing Dynasty, the emperor formally granted the title to Dalai Lama V in the name of the central political power. Later, over a transitional period of nearly 100 years, the Dalai Lama and Panchen Lama were not only the spiritual leaders of the Tibetan people, but controlled the politics, economy and defence of Tibet as well.

Tibetan Buddhism also differs in that it is believed in by all Tibetans. In 1950, there were over 5,000 lamaseries in Tibet. Of the Tibetan population, one in ten had a religious profession. In specific regions, half of the male population held office in monasteries, and chanting scriptures and worshipping Buddha became an indispensable part of most people's lives. Tibetan Buddhism has a strong mysterious flavour. Theoretically, though it advocates the practice of both tantric and exoteric religions, it lays emphasis on the practice of tantric dharma, a mysterious and unfathomable religion, paying attention to actual practice and method of passing on from a master to a single disciple, never to an outsider. it differs from the Buddhism of the interior in its over-elaborate and meticulous theory and commandments.

After the reforms carried out by Zong Khaba, the royal court of the Qing government granted special honours to Lamaism, holding it in high esteem. The Dalai Lama and Panchen Lama were invited to the capital on several occasions. Not only were many Lamaist temples built in the outlying regions in the northwest and Inner Mongolia, but even in the imperial gardens of Beijing and Chengde, and the houses lived in by Emperor Yongzheng turned into a lamasery, an example being the Palace of Harmony (Lama Temple), after his death.

1,300 years have passed since the birth of Tibetan Buddhism, and apart from the 100 years during which its followers were persecuted by Langdama, its development has been continuous. Many lamaseries were built all over the Tibetan plateau, and include the magnificent Sangye Monastery built under Lianhuasheng and the sacred palaces that appeared during the rule of Songzan Gampu in Lhasa, the Dazhao, Xiaozhao and Saja monasteries built during the later stage of expansion, Baiju Monastery, Zhashilunpu Monastery and the three big monasteries in Lhasa (Gandan, Zhebang and Sela). In different ways, all these monastic buildings are architectural jewels, the most magnificent, Potala Palace, perched on top of the Red Mountain in Lhasa. Seen by few, they house priceless treasures; Buddhas, mural paintings, Tangka, musical instruments and statues, and constitute an important part of the cultural heritage of China.

The Founding and Evolution of the Buddhist Monastery in China
—— From the Establishment of the Baima Temple to the Forest-like Buddhist Monasteries of the Sui and Tang Dynasties

Buddhist architecture did not at first possess a style of its own, and most monasteries were originally official mansions donated by high-ranking officials and merchants. The very early Baima Monastery, for instance, was a converted government office (Honglusi). Gradually, however, as Buddhism spread into China and merged with Confucianism, monastery building began to take place on a large scale and developed its own style. Characteristics were single-story and storeyed buildings, close eaves, the diamond throne and other versions of towers as well as a layout on a vertical axis. Chinese Buddhist architecture, like that of palace halls and houses, employed the traditional wooden structure, encased by bricks and stones.

In Tibet and the west of Sichuan Province, however, some lamaseries were built using a free layout, and rocks from the vicinity were used, giving the buildings a rich local flavour.

Temple Gate of the Baima Monastery

About 12 km east of Luoyang City in Henan Province stands an ancient monastery, the Baima (white horse) Monastery. Located at the foot of Mt.Wangshan and looking south to the Luohe River, this Buddhist building and pagoda nestle among the green pines and convey a solemn, quiet and secluded atmosphere. Its temple gate is in the style of memorial archway architecture. The horizontal inscribed board was inlaid in the 35th year of the reign of Jiaqing (1556) of the Ming Dynasty, when the gate was rebuilt.

I. The Origin of the Monastery

"Sangharama" is a Sanskrit word, its transliteration being "Sangaromo" or, simplified, "Sangaran." Its original meaning is "the site of a Buddhist house." Later, it became the general term for land on which Buddhist dwelling houses stood and for the buildings on the land,what we would in fact today call a monastery.

In the Chinese written language, the original meaning of "si" (temple) was an ancient government office, for instance the government office in charge of court sacrificial rites was called Honglusi; the office in charge of the choice of scholars and the ceremonies surrounding the ancestral shrine of a ruling house was called Taichangsi. As mentioned above, in the initial stages of Buddhism in China, no monastery building per se existed, and when foreign monks came to the capital they were generally put up at Honglusi. Later, places where monks worshipped Buddha and read the scriptures were also called "si". With the development of Buddhism in China, the form Buddhist temples took quickly increased and the buildings were given different names.

In the 7th year of the reign of Yongping (64), Emperor Mingdi of the Eastern Han Dynasty, the emperor sent Cai Yin, Qin Jing and others to Tianzhu to seek dharma and compile "*the Examples of Buddha*." In the 10th year of Yongping, together with the Indian Buddhist monks Niemoteng and Zhufalan, they turned back to Luoyang and were put up at Honglusi, the guest house of the time. In the 11th year of Yongping, due to the Buddhist scriptures having been carried on the back of a white horse, the place where they were put up was called Baima (white horse) Monastery, the earliest to be recorded.

The Baima Monastery of today is to be found in a stretch of cypress forest 12.5 km east of Luoyang in Henan Province. According to historical records, it was completed during the reign of Chuigong (685-688) of Wu Zetian of the Tang Dynasty. At that time, there were 1,000 monks in the monastery. It was rebuilt during the reign of Chunhua (990-994) of the Song Dynasty. After further large scale renovation, it looked all the more like a heavenly palace. In later generations, it was repaired and some new buildings were added in the Jin (1115-1234), Yuan (1206-1368), Ming (1368-1644) and Qing (1616-1911) dynasties.

It is said that then the Baima Monastery was built in Indian style. It had a nine-storeyed Shelimu stupa and the halls were decorated with murals. The present monastery mostly reflects the appearance it took on after the rebuilding

Qingliang Terrace in the Baima Monastery

To the rear of the central axis of the Baima Monastery, there is a brick-paved high terrace known as the Qingliang (cooling) Terrace. It is the earliest architectural site still extant. Standing at 6 m, the terrace is 42.8 m long from east to west and 32.4 m wide from south to north.

in the 52nd year of Emperor Kangxi (1713) of the Qing Dynasty. On the central axis are: the Hall of the Heavenly King, the Hall of the Big Buddha, the Precious Hall of the Great Hero and four main reception halls.

Though the Baima Monastery has been rebuilt many times, the site of the monastery remains unchanged to this day. The Qingliang Platform, the Ganlujing (Sweet dew well), and the Scripture-burning Platform preserved since the Han Dynasty are still faintly visible.

II. The Structural Evolution of the Chinese Monastery

In the early years of Indian Buddhism, monks propagated Buddhism while travelling. As time passed, instead of travelling they settled at different places, and their provisional dwelling places developed into Buddhist monasteries for religious meetings and Buddhist ceremonies. Jingshe (spiritual dwelling) was a kind of Buddhist house, serving at first as living quarters. Later, large-scale monastic buildings came into being for use by groups of monks, Zhuyuan Jingshe (bamboo garden spiritual dwelling), built and presented by the rich and powerful Galanto and Luoyang Jingshe, built by the elder Jushilu of Bacuo state, being examples. The most famous was Zhiyuan Jingshe in Shewei City, a well-appointed and well-organized Buddhist monastery. It is said that before the birth of Sakya, it had 16 extensive courtyards, each with over 60 dwellings for the monks.

When Buddhism was propagated in China, foreign monks brought along with them Buddhist scriptures and religious doctrines, but the Indian pagoda or stupa was not introduced at the same time.

On the advent of Buddhism, China already possessed highly unique forms of architecture. It is not to be denied that Buddhism, introduced from India via the western regions, led to new impulses in the fields of architecture and art, but as they met with a strong and highly developed native culture, these new influences led to a Buddhist art and architectural style that had Chinese modifications.

The centre of traditional Buddhist monasteries in India was occupied by a stupa, and this in turn was surrounded by typical Buddhist houses. Monasteries in the early years of Buddhism in China were given a corridor and courtyard. The end of 200 A.D. saw the large-scale erection of Stupa memorial temples due to the initiative of Zha Rong, a citizen of Danyang, who collected money from three prefectures in Xuzhou in Jiangsu Province. The top of the Stupa was embellished with gold plating, and below were storeyed buildings surrounded by halls and pavilions. The fact that such edifices could hold 3,000 people gives one an idea of their scale.

The period of the Northern and Southern Dynasties was a time when it became fashionable to give up one's dwelling so that it could serve as a monastery. The reasons differed, and in some cases, committing a crime led to people's houses being searched and confiscated by the authorities and turned into a monastery. Others became monks themselves and donated their property to the monastery. Others again were high officials and noblemen who believed that contributing their large houses to the monastery would bring them good fortune and avert disaster. This widespread habit meant that the monastery itself was basically of a Chinese style that had been prevalent since the Han Dynasty (206-220). Both Chinese traditional dwellings and altar temples had halls for sacrifices at their centre, and extending outwards in succession a courtyard and winding corridor. As a result, the monastery turned its corridor-courtyard layout into one on a central axis, the centre being taken up by the Buddhist hall.

In addition to the above-mentioned reasons for giving up one's dwelling to serve as monastery, nobles within the imperial family, those of royal descent and celebrities with no official posts were also eager to build monasteries. Yao Xing of the Late Zhao state started to have stupa erected at Yongguili and a platform made of huge stones. Mount Sumeru stood at the centre surrounded by lofty ridges and towering cliffs. Rare birds and animals were to be found in the lavish forests, as well as celestial beings and Buddhist statues. Yang Xianzhi of the Northern Wei wrote in *"the Story of Buddhist Temples in Luoyang"* describing the rise and fall of over 40 temples in Luoyang, capital of the Northern Wei Dynasty, that the biggest in scale was Yongning Monastery. "In the monastery there is a nine-storeyed pagoda. A wooden structure, it is 90 zhang (297 m) high with a spire of 10 zhang (about 30 m).... One can see it 100 li (50 km) away from the capital. To the north of the pagoda, there is a Buddhist hall taking the form of the Supreme Ultimate Hall. A giant gold statue 1.8 zhang (about 6 m) high stands there." The whole monastery was magnificent in scale. Its plan was square in shape and the whole was surrounded by a wall. On top of this rafters were installed, covered with tiles like a palace wall of the time. There were gates on four sides. The southern gate-tower was similar in style to that of the southern main entrance to the city of Luoyang in that it had three storeys and three successive doors. The eastern and western gates also had three successive doors but were only two-storeyed, and the northern gate only had one storey. Chinese scholar trees grew along the surrounding wall, along which ran a stretch of greenish water. In the centre of the monastery stood a huge pagoda of nine storeys. On top of it and on the eave-corners hung 120 golden bells, "a high wind blows throughout the night, the treasured bells ring together." To the north of the pagoda was a large Buddhist hall and over 1,000 Buddhist houses. This arrangement of pagoda in the centre with Buddhist houses all around was the result of Indian influence. However, the square shape with gates on four sides was the result of the merging of ritual Han Dynasty architecture with that of Buddhist architecture, and as such, the Yongning Monastery is an outstanding example of the combination of Chinese and western elements.

By the time of the Sui and Tang dynasties, Buddhism in China was undergoing unprecedented development, and temples were being built on a large scale. The form the temple layout now took was a courtyard surrounded by dwellings as a unit, and multi-courtyards forming different combinations. Some big monasteries had over 10 courtyards, such as the Ci'en Monastery in Chang'an built during the Tang Dynasty.

The vertical axis arrangement came in the end to be the definitive layout for the Buddhist monastery in China, whereby the main halls were arranged on the central axis. Large-scale temples were located on both sides thus forming further axes parallel to each other for the siting of subsidiary halls and Buddhist dwellings. This layout still exists today. The Xinglong Monastery in Zhengding County in Hebei Province, built in the Song Dynasty (960-1279), and the Zhihua

**Moni Hall in the Longxing
Monastery**

Moni Hall is an extremely important
Buddhist building in the Longxing
Monastery. The great hall is rectangular in
shape. Its four sides were each provided
with a veranda, thus giving the building
a cross-shape. The great hall is double-
eaved with sloped roofing. Except for the
four verandas that have each been given
a door, the other sides are all constructed
with thick, windowless walls.

Monastery in Beijing were examples of this central axis layout. Located at Lumicang in Beijing, the Zhihua Monastery was first built in the 8th year of the reign of Zhengtong (1443) by the eunuch Wang Zhen. This monastery has been renovated several times and was added to at the end of the Ming Dynasty and in the first years of the Qing Dynasty. The whole monastery was arranged from south to north, dividing into three left, central and right lines and divided by two paved passageways. As most buildings owned by the nobility were arranged on three axis lines, paralleling on a plan, the monastery very likely derived from former mansions. Today, the buildings on the east and west two lines no longer exist, the halls on the central axis remain intact. From south to north in succession are: the temple gate, Zhihua gate, Zhihua Hall and Rulai (Tathagata) Hall (Zhihua Tower of Ten-thousand Buddhas), forming three courtyards. Behind Rulai Hall is a dividing wall, and entering the central gate, there is a subsidiary courtyard consisting of Dabei Hall, Wanfa Hall and abbots' rooms. Compared with the strict symmetric layout, it has a more flexible and diversified look about it.

III. The Transformation and Evolution of the Pagoda

The Buddhist pagoda originated from India, and in Sanskrit, it is called "stupa". In Chinese its transliteration is "cui du po". It was originally a grave or tomb for the dead. It was first built of earth and brick, and its external appearance resembled a pan bottom upside-down. Later, it gradually developed into a solid structure composed of base, inverted alms bowl, treasure box and Wheel of the Law. It is said that after Buddha passed away, his body was cremated and luminous pearls emerged from the ash. These relics were divided into several parts and pagodas were separately built to protect them. Up to the beginning of the Christian era, the stupa base gradually increased to contain two or three steps. The Wheel of the Law increased to 11 in number and its form and structure became tall and slender. A shrine room could also be built in the inverted alms bowl to enshrine and worship Buddha or Buddhist objects.

In India there was another kind of Buddhist pagoda called "chaitya," set in a small memorial temple in stone caves for monks to perform religious services or offer sacrifices. When the chaitya was introduced into China, it was set up in the centre of stone caves, and the upper part of the pagoda was connected with the cave top, forming a pagoda pillar.

India Buddhist monasteries used the pagoda as centre with Buddhist houses built all around. After Buddhism was introduced into China, pagodas were in the initial stages also built in the centre of the monastery. Cases in point are the Yongning Monastery in Luoyang in Henan Province and the Fogong Monastery in Yingxian County of Shanxi Province. As Chinese Buddhism developed from studying scripture to sacrificing to Buddha, temple pagodas were gradually moved to the rear or to the east and west ends of the monastery. Later, they were even moved out of the temple, either perched on the top of a mountain or made to look down at level farmland often in conjunction with green waters. The different shadows thrown by the pagoda on such a gentle and smooth horizon delineates just those beautiful contours unique to ancient Chinese architecture.

After the pagoda was introduced into China, various styles were established, all in keeping with the given Chinese architectural tradition, such as the tower-styled pagoda, the pagoda with close eaves, the pavilion-style pagoda, the diamond-throne pagoda, the lama pagoda, the flower pagoda, the overhead pagoda spanning a lane, the pagoda containing the treasure box inscribed with scripture and others. The Chinese pagoda affords from its summit impressive views of the surrounding countryside, thus furthering its function.

The tower-styled pagoda   There are two different versions of this kind of pagoda, in wood and in stone. Well-preserved and the most prolific, it is the model of the Chinese-style Buddhist pagoda. In the early years, most tower-styled pagodas were of wooden structure and tall in shape. They were the most common type during the Northern and Southern Dynasties. According

Xiaoyan Pagoda in the Jianfu Monastery

Located on the central axis of the Jianfu Monastery, the Xiaoyan (lesser wild goose) pagoda is square in shape with close eaves. Only thirteen of the original 15 storeys are extant. The distance between them is at first considerable, getting less and less so as the pagoda rises upwards, its diameter decreasing in such a way that the structure takes on a gradual curved effect.

Zhenguo Pagoda of the Kaiyuan Monastery

On the east and west sides of the Kaiyuan Monastery in Quanzhou stands a tower-like pagoda. Octagonal in shape, the five-storeyed pagodas were built in the style of a wooden structure. The Zhenguo Pagoda is on the eastern side. Built of granite, it is 48.24 m high, and each storey has four doors and four windows. Those of the neighbouring storeys are staggered so that they do not appear on the same side. Statues of warriors, heavenly kings, arhats and others decorate both sides of these openings. Inside, an octagonal pillar soars upward.

to historical documents, the Futu Monastery in Xuzhou of the Eastern Han Dynasty and the Yongning Monastery in Luoyang of the Northern and Southern Dynasties both had wooden tower pagodas. As the wooden structure and framework were easily destroyed by fire, the only old and well-preserved extant example is in the Fogong Monastery in Yingxian County of Shanxi Province, built during the Liao Dynasty. After the Tang Dynasty, tower-styled pagodas of wooden structure had become the main pagoda style. At the time, stone and brick piling skill had reached a very high standard, and stone and brick pagodas in various complicated styles were built. Shapes for the stone and brick pagoda were many, such as quadrilateral, hexagonal, octagonal and others. The pagoda was provided with stairs so that people could go up and down. The external appearance of the pagoda is characterized by windows, round pillars, square pillars, dougong brackets and eaves formed by using wooden moulds. The treatment of interior space varied: the tubular pagoda such as the Dayan Pagoda in Xi'an in Shaanxi Province; the solid pagoda such as the Flying Rainbow Pagoda in Hongtong County of Shanxi Province; the central-pillared pagoda such as the Renshou Pagoda in Kaiyuan of Quanzhou in Fujian Province; the tubular pagoda with an internal tubular construction such as the Yunyan Pagoda in Suzhou in Jiangsu Province being examples.

The close-eave pagoda   Also built of stone and brick, the first storey of the pagoda is very tall, providing the principal surface for decoration with Buddhist statues, Lokapalas (gigantic statues standing inside the entrance of Buddhist temple), lotus flowers and geometric patterns; doors, windows and pillars all providing additional forms of decoration. Above the second storey, the pagoda eaves pile up one on top of another, and there are no doors and windows. Most close-eave pagodas are solid and cannot be ascended. The pagoda in the Songyue Monastery in Henan Province, the Xiaoyan (lesser wild goose) Pagoda in Xi'an in Shaanxi Province, the Qianxun Pagoda in the Chongsheng Monastery of Dali, Yunnan Province, are all excellent examples of close-eave pagodas in existence today.

The pavilion-styled pagoda   Most are single storey and can be square, hexagonal or octagonal in shape. Generally, they serve as tombs for the monks. The posthumous Zushi (Founder) pagoda of the Tang Dynasty in the Fuoguang Monastery of Mount Wutai in Shanxi Province is one of the well-known pavilion-styled pagodas still in existence today.

The diamond-throne pagoda   The lower part of the pagoda consists of a huge base, known as the diamond throne. The throne (base) is sculptured with fine Buddhist statues and patterns. The lower part of the throne has a door and on top of the throne five small pagodas stand, the central one slightly larger than the others, and housing five Buddhist relics of the Tantra Sect. This kind of pagoda is represented by the Zhengjue Monastery and the Biyun Monastery pagodas in Beijing. There also exists another kind of flower pagoda, the forerunner of the diamond throne pagoda, an example being the Guanghui Monastery flower pagoda in Hebei Province, built during the Jin Dynasty.

The dagoba   Also known as the inverted alms bowl pagoda, its lower part forms the foundation, the pagoda then tapering upwards storey by storey. The

foundation of the large dagoba is quite tall, and it is topped by a semi-circular
construction resembling an inverted alms bowl, its obvious forerunner the stupa
of India. On top of the inverted alms bowl is the pagoda body, consisting of the
Sumeru throne, the thirteen days (Wheel of the Law), the canopy and crown.
The earliest Chinese dagoba still in existence is the Miaoying Monastery white
pagoda built in the 8th year of the reign of Zhiyuan (1271) of the Yuan Dynasty.
The square pagoda foundation is nine metres high, and the pagoda body itself
of solid appearance. Sculptures depicting the story of Buddha's life decorate the
base of the Zhangjia living Buddha Pagoda in the Zhenhai Monastery of Mount
Wutai in Shanxi Province. The pagoda was built in the 51st year of the reign of
Emperor Qianlong (1786) of the Qing Dynasty.

IV. The Stone Cave Monastery

The building of stone cave monasteries originated in India. Early on during
the Maurya Empire (321-187 B.C.), members of the rich and powerful royal

family of Anda had caves dug in mountain cliffs for Buddhist monks. Stone cave monasteries in India can generally be divided into two kinds, the vihara and the chaitya. The former was square-shaped with small shrines dug out on three sides for the monks to pray to Buddha, live and rest. The latter was U-shaped with stupas erected in the centre and to the rear. Religious ceremonies took place in the cave.

Stone cave monasteries were introduced into China via the Western Regions during the Eastern Han Dynasty (25-220 A.D.), and geographically, they were located chiefly in the western parts of China. In Xinjiang alone, there were over 100 stone caves scattered over 10 localities. Historically, stone cave monasteries began to be built successively during the Eastern Han Dynasty. The peak period for the building of stone cave monasteries lasted from the Northern and Southern Dynasties up to those of the Sui and Tang. After that there was a decline. Functionally, stone cave monasteries could be divided into the following categories: one kind served as the place for monks to live in and practise Buddhism, and generally they were small, examples being Cave No.

22 in Yungang in Shanxi Province and some small caves to the north of the Mogao Cave in Gansu Province. In Cave No. 285 of Dunhuang, stone rooms were dug out around its central hall for monks to perform Buddhist ceremonies. Another kind of Buddhist hall served as a place for monks to hold religious services. Some had a carved-out shrine for a Buddhist statue. Still others had a pagoda in the centre of the stone cave, where Buddhist relics were kept. The cave walls were sculptured with Buddhas, and in front of the Buddhist statue and the pagoda, there was space for worshipping and chanting prayers. Stone caves were dug out purely to house large Buddhist statues, examples being Kezhir cave in Xinjiang, Cave Nos. 16-20 in Yungang, the Fengxian Monastery in Longmen and others. Huge Buddhas were even sculpted outside in the open and were much revered by visitors. The giant Buddha of the Lingyun Monastery in Leshan, Sichuan Province first began to be carved in the first year of the reign of Kaiyuan (1713), Emperor Xuanzong of the Tang Dynasty, and took 90 years. Early on, it was covered by a seven-storey tower. This giant Buddha faces the confluence of the three rivers, Qingyi, Minjiang and Dadu. With a shoulder width of 24 metres, the sitting Buddha is 71 metres tall, and represents one of the largest stone-sculpted statues in the world.

The Kezhir stone cave   The earliest carved-out stone cave still in existence in China is the Kezhir Thousand Buddhas Cave in Baicheng City in Xinjiang. It is located on the northern bank of the Muzhati River, east of the city. Now there are 263 caves, representing the largest stone cave group dating from the era of the ancient Qiuci city state of the Western Regions. The Kezhir stone cave monastery was first built from the 3rd to the beginning of the 4th century. Those excavated in the early years were chiefly big Buddhist statue caves, the statues ranging from a height of several metres to a score or more. These stone caves were mostly copied from those of India. Still in existence are a large number of mural paintings on Hinayana Buddhist themes.

The Mogao Cave   The Mogao Cave in Dunhuang in Gansu Province was first built in 400 A.D. The earliest still in existence are the few caves excavated in the Northern Liang, chiefly housing a single Buddha. These statues were strongly moulded, the forehead broad, the eyes large, the nose straight and the lips thin. The clothing was of Persian and India style, the influence here of the Western Regions being obvious. In the stone caves dating from the Northern Wei Dynasty (386-534), groups of Buddhist statues began to appear. The rich, artistic elements typical of the Central Plains manifested themselves in these

Front Corridor of Cave No. 11 of the Tianlong Mountain Stone Caves

The Tianlong Mountain stone cave complex, in Taiyuan, Shanxi Province, comprises altogether 21 caves, and other minor ones, including statues of the Eastern Wei (534-550), the Northern Qi (550-577), the Sui, Tang and the Five dynasties (907-960). To be seen here are the cave eaves and square pillars, tall and slender in proportion. The entrance to the cave takes the form of an arched gate, above which is a flame-shaped relief.

statues, with their oval-shaped faces, smooth eyebrows and expressive eyes. The group of stone caves based on the Mogao Cave spreads out over a cliff face, stretching for 1,600 m from south to north and including more than 490 caves containing 2,200 coloured Buddhist statues and expansive mural paintings. These caves, created over a period of more than 1,000 years and covering more than ten dynasties are indeed a rare and precious heritage.

The Yungang Stone Cave   The Yungang Stone Cave was first built during the reign of Emperor Wencheng (452-464) of the Northern Wei Dynasty. It took 35 years to finish. Now there are 53 caves in existence containing 51,000 Buddhist statues. Among them the most magnificent were the five stone caves dug out and decorated by TanYao. It is said that these caves were built to pray for the happiness of the five emperors after Emperor Gaozu. Oval in plan, the rear wall was taken up by a huge Buddhist statue. The statues in the Yungang Stone Caves were noticeably influenced by the Buddhist art of India. In addition to the five caves by TanYao, there are also two kinds of cave forms, the one square in plan, the other divided into front and rear rooms. The inner wall of the cave is fully carved with relief sculptures of Buddha. In those years, the emperor of the Northern Wei Dynasty often went on an inspection tour to Yungang, a well-known meeting place for many eminent monks and an important centre for the translation of scripture during the Northern Wei Dynasty.

The Longmen Stone Cave   Along the banks of the River Yihe in Yinan, Luoyang (Henan Province) over 1,300 caves were excavated and filled with nearly 100,000 Buddhist statues. This is the Longmen Stone Cave famous the world over . It was first built in 500 A.D. The Fengxian Monastery represents the largest of the stone caves in Longmen, and the Buddhist statue it contains is 17 m high.

The Maijishan Stone Cave　In the Qinling mountain range, west of Tianshui in Gansu Province, there is a solitary peak, which on account of its wheat stack shape, is called Maijishan (the wheat stack mountain). The caves were dug along a sheer precipice, one on top of the other, in disorderly profusion, up and down, and were connected with zigzag plank roadways. The whole peak is divided into two, the east cliff and the west cliff. With its nearly 200 caves and more than 7,000 statues and clay mouldings, Maijishan represents one of the caves with the greatest number of statues in China.

During the Northern and Southern Dynasties, Buddhism in the Northern Dynasty had a strong political element, religious and state power being closely united. During the time of the emperor of Mingyuan of the Northern Wei Dynasty, the Buddhist monk Faguo put forward that his majesty was the Tathagata of the present time...... worshipping the Son of Heaven meant

External View of the Maijishan Stone Caves

The Maijishan Stone Caves were carved out of a sheer precipice following the geological features. The caves were thus linked by planks fixed to the perpendicular rock faces by means of wooden brackets. It is the only stone cave monastery to literally cling to a precipice, and as such is a breathtaking architectural achievement.

worshipping Buddha. This naturally implied a strengthening of the political status of Buddhism in the Northern Dynasty. Monks were officially exhorted to guide the people, the state thus benefiting from Buddhism, as Buddhism benefited from the state. The emperor for his part interfered directly in the building of monasteries and those in stone caves and the excavation of all the large groups of stone caves in the north was directly linked with the imperial family.

V. The Building of the Lamasery

Tibetan Buddhist monasteries are commonly called lamaseries and are very different in style from those of the interior. Especially the lamaseries of the Qinghai-Tibet Plateau and the northwest have a distinctive style of their own. From the time Songzan Gampu built the first group of sacred halls--- the Dazhao Monastery, the Xiaozhao Monastery and Potala Palace --- to the 11th century A.D., various Tibetan Buddhist sects had become established in succession. Lamaseries began to be built on a large scale. In addition to the three big monasteries in Lhasa, lamaseries, big and small, spread all over Tibet, their architecture expressing the essence of Tibetan wisdom.

The Sangye Monastery　　The first Lamaist monastery, it was initially built in the middle of the 8th century A.D., and was later rebuilt during the time of Dalai VII. Its main Buddhist halls were all built within the circular surrounding wall, and in the centre stands the Big Hall of Wuce. The 12 halls around symbolize the four greater continental parts and the eight lesser ones in the saltwater around Mt. Sumeru. At the four corners stand four relic pagodas in white, green, turquoise and red, symbolizing the Four Heavenly Kings. To the south and north are the Sun Hall and Moon Hall. The circular stone wall symbolizes the periphery of the world. The overall arrangement of the Sangye Monastery is based completely on Buddhism's concept of the world. It is the most unusual example of layout among the lamaseries in Tibet. In the 20th year of Emperor Qianlong (1755) of the Qing Dynasty, the Puning Monastery was built in Chengde, Hebei Province to commemorate the suppression of the Dawaqi rebellion in Zhun'ger. The principal hall, Mahauana Tower, was built along the lines of the Big Hall of Wuce in the Sangye Monastery.

The Dazhao Monastery　　There are many lamaseries in Tibet, but from the point of view of location and layout of the buildings, they may roughly be divided into two categories: Those in the open country and those in the

Northern View of Potala Palace

Potala Palace is located on the Red Mountain northwest of Lhasa City. A beautiful stretch of water, the so-called Dragon King Pool, lies at the foot of the mountain, behind the palace. It was dug out of lowland left after the building of Potala Palace, which required a huge amount of manpower and material resources. The Red Palace alone took 2130,000 liang (a unit of weight for silver) of silver. The Dragon King Palace was built by the 6th generation of the Dalai.

mountains, an example of the former being the Dazhao Monastery, first built in 467 and at that time part of the Turpan Palace built by Songzan Gampu. The scale of construction was not large, the building in fact being only a part of the Xinjuekang main hall in the present monastery and serving to enshrine and worship the Buddhist statue brought by Princess Wencheng from the Han territory. It was later extended in the Yuan, Ming and Qing dynasties, and especially during the time of Dalai V Lhosang Jiatso (1617-1682), was rebuilt and widely extended, basically forming the present layout. The layout is asymmetric. The main hall stands in the centre with Buddhist hall, scripture hall and various subsidiary houses placed irregularly all round. Juekang main hall is the Buddhist hall for enshrining and worshipping the Buddhist statue. In front of the main hall is the corridor courtyard, around this a wide corridor supported by square pillars. The inner wall of the corridor is fully painted with murals depicting the story of the Thousand Buddhas. In the southern courtyard and on both sides of the main entrance are the living Buddha's government office, the scripture school, the storehouse, the kitchen as well as the local Tibetan government office. The Dazhao Monastery is not purely a religious building, not only a symbol of theocracy, but also centre of political power, fully reflecting the intertwinement of politics and religion characteristic of Tibetan Buddhism. Around the outskirts of the monastery are the inner, central and outer scripture rotating roads for worshipping, known as Langkuo, Bakuo and Linkuo by the local people. The central road for worship later developed into the main commercial street (Baguo Street), and the area surrounded by Linkuo, is the old Lhasa city.

Potala Palace Another kind of lamasery was built on mountain peaks or on mountain slopes and arranged according to the topography. Potala Palace and the three big monasteries in Lhasa are the outstanding representatives of this kind of architecture. The former was first built in the 7th century A.D. and was the palace hall for Princess Wencheng, built by Songzan Ganpu. Later, it was completely destroyed except for a cave for practising Buddhism and a Guanyin hall. From the 17th century A.D., Potala Palace was twice rebuilt and greatly extended by Dalai V and XIII, taking on the appearance it has today. Located on the peak of Hongshan Mountain northwest of Lhasa, Potala Palace was given a free layout. Its principal building had 13 storeys reaching a height of 117 m. It was 400 m wide from east to west, overlooking Lhasa city in the south. In 1645 Dalai V undertook expansions lasting eight years, and finished part of the White Palace. The highest storey in the eastern part of this building was taken up by the sleeping quarters of Dalai. Because it enjoyed sunshine all day long, it was also called the Hall of Sunshine. Here were Dalai Lama's scripture hall, bedroom, guest room and rooms for other activities. In the last years of the Dalai, the building of the Red Palace was commenced and completed in 1693. Of all the treasures here, the spiritual pagoda of Dalai V is the most impressive. Reaching a height of 14 m, 119,000 liang of gold and 4000 pearls were used in the creation of this outstanding work of art. At the foot of the mountain, south of Potala Palace, was the seat of the local administrative organ, including a prison, printing house, as well as other buildings. The east, west and south slopes were surrounded by the palace wall. On the northern face of Hongshan Mountain was a quiet and secluded garden, known as the Pool of the Dragon King and consisting of the Dragon King Palace and the Big Elephant House. Potala Palace occupies 41 ha of land. Magnificent and majestic in appearance, it symbolizes the ethnic spirit, wisdom and artistic achievements of Tibet.

No matter which one chooses, Potala Palace where the Dalai Lama lived or the Zhashilumpu where the Panchen Lama lived, the Saja Monastery in

Lateral View of Dahong Platform in the Xumifushou Monastery

Dahong Platform consists of a three storeyed-tower, Miaogao Zhuangyan Hall, enclosed by another three-storeyed group tower on four sides, a smaller square within a larger one. The wall is inserted with rectangular windows, with highly decorative overhangs. The central entrance on the southern side has a glazed door and is approached by steps leading to it from the east and west. The top of Dahong Platform is flat, and at each of the four corners is a small tower-like building with a single eave.

The Hall of the Anyuan Monastery

The plan of the three-storeyed Hall of Pudu (delivering all from torment) is square. The roof has black glazed titles and a yellow rim. The central ridge is decorated with three bell-shaped dagobas. The vast hall has 32 gold pillars and in its centre a wood-sculptured statue of Ludum is enshrined.

Houzang, the Sanye Monastery in Shannan or the three famous monasteries in Lhasa, architecturally, all gradually absorbed the skill and artistry of the Han nationality. For example, in structure they adopted the traditional Tibetan wood pillar, close-eaves and flat top but at the same time also used the dougong brackets and sloping roof of the Han style. As a result of this blend of artistic details, a brilliant architectural style with distinctive plateau characteristics finally established itself.

As already mentioned, the Tibetan lamasery fulfilled both a religious and political function, and because of this, its scale was larger than that of the monasteries of the interior. The three monasteries in Lhasa are a good example, each having the characteristics of a small town, which, from a distance, could be seen spreading out all over a given mountain slope. Each monastery comprised several large Buddhist halls as well as two or three scripture halls, the largest capable of holding thousands of people. Cuoqin great hall, for example, in the Zhebang Monastery covered an area of 2,000 m². These scripture halls had their walls decorated with murals depicting the life of Buddha, and streamers provided colour in what was otherwise a dark hall with only a skylight to allow a shaft of light to illuminate the Buddhist statue. The small lamps burning continuously in front of the statue and the general gloom lent the whole a mysterious and almost oppressive atmosphere rarely witnessed in the monasteries of the Han territory. The Kangcun village, with its small, winding streets provided accommodation for the lamas but also had administrative offices. The Tibetan monastery represented the centre of the religious life of the society and as such was to be found in almost every place of habitation.

After the Yuan Dynasty (1206-1368), lamaseries began to be built in the northwest, as well as around the capital city. The Ta'er Monastery in Huangzhong County, Qinghai Province, was built in memory of the Great Master Zong Khaba, who was born there. The whole monastery had the memorial pagoda of Zong Khaba (also known as the Hall of Greater Gold Tiles) as its centre, and surrounding this were a Buddhist hall, a scripture hall, a school, a Buddhist pagoda, the Living Buddha's government office, monks' dwellings and many other Buddhist buildings, all forming a large complex. The

The Precious Hall of the Great Hero in the Puning Monastery

The base of the hall is formed by the 1.4 m high Sumeru throne. A platform, approached from the south by three flights of steps, from the east and west by a single flight, was set in front of the hall which has double eaves and a sloping roof of yellow glazed tiles, the borders of the roof in green. The ridge is set off by a glittering bronze relic pagoda.

Labuleng Monastery in Xiahe County, Gansu Province is a lamasery complex combining the architectural styles of the Han and Tibet. The big Zhacangs in the monastery are the highest institutes of Buddhism in southern Gansu.

In the early years of the Qing Dynasty, with the purpose of uniting with the Mongolian and Tibetan ethnic minorities and jointly opposing the invasion by the Russians as well as strengthening the rule of the Qing royal court, twelve monasteries were built on the outskirts of Summer Resort in Chengde. These were the Puren Monastery, the Pushou Monastery, the Puning Monastery, the Anyuan Temple, the Putuozongsheng Monastery, the Shuxiang Temple, the Xumifushou Monastery, the Guangyuan Monastery, the Puyou Monastery, the Pule Monastery, the Guang'an Monastery and Arahat Hall. Of these, the last three were not for lamas, and the other nine belonged to the government office in charge of vassal affairs and had offices in the capital (the Puyou and Puning monasteries had one office in common). As all these monasteries were built outside the capital, they were usually called Waibamiao (the outer eight

Ta'er Monastery

Covering an area of 600 mu (40 hectares), the Ta'er Monastery is a religious township. Its Buddhist buildings are arranged along the valley in a free layout. The principal buildings include a memorial tower, a dharma-protecting hall, a great scripture hall, four scripture academies, the Living Buddha's government office and monks' dwellings.

The Mural Festival in Potala Palace

The mural paintings in Potala Palace include the joyous rendering of a Tibetan folk festival. To be seen here is the festival falling on the 30th day of the 2nd month of the Tibetan calendar. It is a joyous scene, illustrating in a realistic manner how such festivals were celebrated.

Mural Painting of the Sangye Monastery in Potala Palace

In the Potala Palace, there is a mural painting of the Sanye Monastery which was the earliest Lamaist monastery in Tibet. The mural vividly depicts the general layout of the monastery according to the interpretation of the world by Buddhism.

monasteries), their architectural style absorbing the details of well-known monastic architecture in Tibet, Xinjiang, Inner Mongolia, as well as areas around the provinces of Jiangsu and Zhejiang. It has already been mentioned that the Puning Monastery was built according to the architectural style of the Sangye Monastery in Tibet, but the Putuozongsheng and Xumifushou monasteries were respectively built according to that of Potala Palace and the Zhashilunpu Monastery in Tibet, and served as a temporary dwelling for the Panchen and Dalai when they came to the capital to have an audience with the emperor. Pudu (deliver all from torment) Hall in the Anyuan Monastery was built in the style of the Gu'erzha Monastery in Yili, Xinjiang. Again, Xuguang Tower in the Pule Monastery resembles the Hall of Prayer for Good Harvests of the Temple of Heaven in Beijing. These eight monasteries, with their rich and colourful architectural style, are a splendid testimony to Lamaist architecture. Still today they attract Buddhist followers and lovers of Buddhist architecture from all over the world.

The Artistic Characteristics of Buddhist Architecture in China
—— The Blending of Western Buddhist Culture and Chinese Innate Culture

The purpose of Buddhist temples in China was mainly to enshrine and worship Buddhist statues, and they generally had a horizontal layout to merge with the prevailing Chinese architecture. Tower-style hall temple is another form existed for the enshrinement and worship of giant statues. In Tibet, the Buddhist monastery also provided amenities for the chanting of scriptures, and was thus much larger in scale, providing space for thousands of lamas to conduct services simultaneously.

In addition to the hall or monastery for the performance of services, there were also pagodas and a pagoda courtyard to the rear or sides. Buildings for meditation, monks' dwellings, guest halls, buildings for housing the scriptures, printing facilities and other subsidiary buildings completed the complex.

The layout of some of the monasteries reflected the Buddhist view of the world. The Sangye Monastery, for instance, in Tibet, mirrors the Buddhist conception of the world's formation. The Puning Monastery in Chengde has four halls symbolizing the Buddhist conception of the continents.

Buddhist architecture also has its particular characteristics. The moulding of the statues, the shapes of the pagoda spires, the mural paintings all testify to the uniqueness of Buddhist art.

I. The Varied Natural Settings Chosen for the Location of the Buddhist Monastery

As a common Chinese proverb has it, "Since ancient times most of the famous mountains have been occupied by monks," the location of many a Chinese monastery is amid beautiful countryside, away from the bustle of cities. Some large monasteries were located on urban sites, attracting large numbers of pilgrims. But the majority of monastic pagodas, temples and, of course, stone cave monasteries were hidden away in green valleys, nestled along the banks of big rivers and lakes or were located on the slopes and peaks of high mountains or on plateaus.

In the early years of the Han Dynasty, it was customary to follow the way of Taoism of the Yellow Emperor and Laotse, but gradually, the practice of worshipping and believing in the Lord of Heaven and the ancestors began to spread. After Emperor Wudi of the Han Dynasty, Confucian thought even became paramount. When Buddhism was first introduced into China, it did not attract the attention of the majority of the lower and middle classes, as those who had contact with monks from the western regions were mostly imperial kinsfolk and upper-class government officials. When Buddhist monasteries began to be built in the Han Dynasty, they served as a place where sacrifices could be made to Buddha for good luck, and also to meet the religious needs of traders coming to China from the western regions. Most monasteries at this time were built in or on the outskirts of cities, or along trading routes leading from the Han territory to the western regions. As Buddhism developed, cities continued to be the ideal location for monasteries as it was easier from there to gain the understanding of rulers for the new religion, and thus increase its influence.

With the establishment of Buddhist sects, and the recognition in particular of the Pure Land and the Chan sects by high officials, the upper-class and the common people, more and more monasteries came to be built in the country,

Manjusri Hall of the Shuxiang Monastery, Mt. Wutai

Manjusri Hall is the principal Buddhist building in the monastery. Five-bays wide, with double-eaves and a sloping roof, it is the largest monastic building in the central area of Mt.Wutai.

59

Statue of Manjusri with the Thousand Alms Bowls in the Xiantong Monastery of Mt. Wutai

Like the statue of the eleven-faced Guanyin, the statue of Manjusri has five heads one on top of the other. In front of his chest are three pairs of big arms, one of which is raised over the head in worship of the sacred statue.

Manjusri Statue in Manjusri Hall, Shuxiang Monastery, Mt. Wutai

Manjusri, also known as the Bodhisattva of supreme wisdom has a full and round face, her ear lobes elongated. On her head is a highly ornate five-Buddha crown and she is presented riding a legendary beast of prey.

actively supported by the imperial rulers. Monks would leave the bustle of the cities for the quiet solitude of the mountains and forests, and devote themselves to the study of Buddhism. Tiantai, Zhongnan, Qixia, Huqiu, Jizu, Yangdang as well as the mountains of Lushan, Hengshan, Langshan and Qianshan all became Buddhist centres, attracting worshippers and travellers from home and abroad. The four mountains, Wutai, Putuo, Emei and Jiuhua too all became world-famous for their Buddhist monasteries.

Wutai Mountain   A mountain range located in the northeast of Wutai County, Shanxi Province, and consisting of five peaks within a circumference of 250 km. In ancient times it was known as Wufeng (five peaks) Mountain and later Qingliang (cooling) Mountain. Versions differ as to when Buddhism established itself in the area, but one knows that monasteries were built there during the Northern Wei Dynasty. After the persecution at the hands of

Dizang Bodhisattva Statue in the Roushen Precious Hall on Mt.Jiuhua

Also known as the Dabei (great sorrow) Bodhisattva, Dizang is one of the four Bodhisattvas. Mt. Jiuhua is where she expounded Buddhist teachings, and the Roushen (the mortal body) Precious Hall is where she attained Buddhahood.

Guanyin Bodhisattva in Yuantong Hall of the Fayu Monastery on Mt. Putuo

Guanyin, Amitaba and Bodhisattva Dashi are the three sages in the West. She is also known as one of the four eminent Bodhisattvas. Guanyin is mostly presented as female in Chinses Buddhist monasteries.

Emperor Wudi of the Northern Zhou (577-581), Buddhism started to flourish again under Emperor Wendi of the Sui Dynasty. An imperial edict was issued whereby a monastery was to be built on each of the five peaks. From then on Wutai prospered and successive emperors of the Song, Yuan, Ming and Qing dynasties commanded that monasteries be built. Investigations in 1956 showed that there were still over 100 monasteries in the area, and it is still today a highly popular place of pilgrimage.

Putuo Mountain　Known as Yongdong in ancient times and located east of Ningbo City, it is one of the most beautiful mountains on the Zhoushan Islands. Later, because Mei Fu of the Western Han Dynasty had been there and tried to have pills of immortality made, it was given the name of Meiling Mountain in the Tang Dynasty. One Buddhist monastery, Meifu Chan Court, still exists. During the reign of Dazhong (847-859) of the Tang Dynasty, foreign

Hall of the Heavenly King in the Fayu Monastery on Mt. Putuo

The monastery itself was built on the sixth storeyed platform. The last of these has an elevation of 23 m above the first courtyard. The hall here was erected on the second platform. Which is 4 m high, and is double-eaved with a sloping roof. A fringer of green tiles skirts the base of the yellow walls.

Temple Gate of the Wannian Monastery on Mount Emei
opposite page

This temple gate of one of the famous ancient monasteries was rebuilt in the 1950s. The monastery was renamed several times during its long history and was given the name it bears today, the Shengshou Wannian Monastery during the reign of Wanli of the Ming Dynasty. It was originally built during the Jin Dynasty and called the Samanthabhandra Monastery, renamed Baishui (white water) Monastery during the Tang Dynasty, reverting to its former name during the Song.

monks came here to perform Buddhist rites, and from then on Putuo Mountain became known throughout the world as the Holy Land where Guanyin (God of Mercy) lived. *The Huayan Scriptures* relate the following, "Lay Buddhist Sebilo instructs Boy Shancai, telling him that in the south there is a mountain called Putan (Putuo) Luojia where there is a Bodhisattva, Guanyin." The mountain was accordingly renamed Putuo Mountain and the small island across the sea to the southeast was called Luojia Mountain.

Putuo Mountain covers an area of less than 13 km^2. The island is long and narrow from north to south and its mountains, with their bizarre peaks, luxuriantly green. Buddhist monasteries and nunneries are dotted all over and it has for centuries been where people have gone to worship and pray to Guanyin Bodhisattva.

Emei Mountain The mountain is located along the southwest border of the Sichuan basin, and because its two peaks resemble the beautiful eyebrows of a woman, it was given the name of Emei. The main peak soars to a height of over 3,000 m, a magnificent sight with tall and graceful ridges and peaks as well

as luxuriant forests. With a circumference of over 110 km^2, the mountains are punctuated with countless monasteries, each, depending on its location, with its own distinctive air. According to *the Huayan Scriptures*, "In the southwest there is a place called the 'Bright Mountain'. Since ancient times, many Bodhisattvas have been living there. Today the Bodhisattva is called Samantabhadra. With her family dependents of 3,000, she often expounds Buddhist teachings on the mountain." Buddhist scholars therefore also called Mount Emei the "Bright Mountain" and honoured it as the place where Samantabhadra performed Buddhist rites. Each monastery has a Samantabhadra hall for worshipping Samantabhadra. During the reign of Emperor Wudi of the Jin Dynasty (256-420), Buddhism spread far and wide and many monasteries were built. In 400 A.D., Huichi, the younger brother of the Pure Land Sect founder Huiyuan, came to Mount Emei, and the first formal monastery, the Samantabhadra Monastery -- the predecessor of the Wannian Monastery -- was built on the mountain. Huichi thus became known as the founder of Mount Emei. Buddhism on Mount Emei enjoyed the generous support of various emperors, from Emperor Taizu Zhu

Yuanzhang to Emperor Shenzong, Zhu Yijun, gaining widespread fame as a centre of Buddhism.

Jiuhua Mountain　Located 20 km southwest of Qingyang County in the south of Anhui Province, it encompassed over 100 km². The name derives from a poem written during the Tang Dynasty by Li Bai, who described the scenery thus, "In the past I stood by the Jiujiang River, gazing at Jiuhua peak in the distance. The heavenly river is hung with green water, its banks embroidered with the cotton rose hibiscus." Monasteries have been built here since the Eastern Jin Dynasty (317-420). In the 4th year of the reign of Yonghui (653) of

Zhiyuan Monastery on Mt.Jiuhua

The Buddhist buildings in the monastery are set out around three courtyards. The front hall is a tower-like three-storeyed building with single eaves and a roof resembling a hilltop. The entrance to the middle courtyard has been given white walls, forming a striking contrast with the red of the tower walls. The rear hall, the Precious hall of the Great Hero, is double-eaved and has sloped roofing. The yellow tiles of the roof are set off by the dark green of the surrounding foliage.

Huacheng Monastery on Mt.Jiuhua

The plan of the monastery shows an axis running through four courtyards. In front of the monastery is a semi-circular pool. The Buddist buildings of the first three courtyards were built in the last years of the Qing Dynasty. The double-eaved great hall with sloped roofing in the last courtyard is only extant building dating from the reign of Wanli of the Ming Dynasty. Green tiles cover the roofs of the halls in the four courtyards. The temple gate of the first courtyard was given the horse-headed walls frequently used in southern Anhui Province. The gables of the other courtyards were given the fire wall style of Zhejiang Province. With its white walls and grey tiles, simple and unadorned, the temple gate has the appearance of a private dwelling.

the Tang Dynasty, Jin Qiaojue, Prince of Xinluo, who had renounced his family and become a monk, came to Jiuhua Mountain by sea. He had the Huacheng Monastery built in the centre of what is nowadays Jiuhua street and settled. When he passed away at the age of 99, his body did not decay and was put in a pagoda, peacefully enshrined in the Roushen (the mortal body) Treasure Hall. Jin Qiaojue's religious name was Dizang. It is said that he was the reincarnation of the Dizang Bodhisattva. Jiuhua Mountain thus became known throughout the world as the place where Dizang Bodhisattva had made his presence felt and expounded Buddhist teachings.

Monasteries therefore were generally located in the vicinity of mountains or rivers, in areas known for the picturesqueness of their scenery. In this, the monks showed that they understood the traditional love the Chinese had always had for nature, and by integrating the monasteries and temples into just the countryside, attracted people to the new religion. The number of those making pilgrimages to these places increased and with it their reverence for Buddhism.

II. The Treatment of Space in the Buddhist Monastery on Han Territory

The Buddhist monastery in China uses the traditional quadrangle layout as its basic component unit. A number of courtyards are arranged along the central axis, which also has the main halls concentrated along it. The large monasteries had other axes leading off from both sides of the central axis, forming units fulfilling different functions.

As the term suggests, the quadrangle is a square courtyard surrounded by buildings on all sides, with a living space in the centre. Some courtyards have buildings on three sides and a wall on the other. Such are the fundamental architectural forms of the Han in China. The typical quadrangle in Beijing has a wall with an ornate gate or guoting (pass-through pavilion) between the southern and the main buildings in the north. The inner courtyard is the main living area. The guest house is situated in the outer courtyard, which is also used for other purposes. Known as 'shangfang,' the main buildings face south and the doors open onto the courtyard. Buildings flanking the east and west are called chambers. Outside the wall with the ornate gate are the southern buildings with rooms facing north. Large dwellings have several courtyards. The main buildings and chambers are connected by winding corridors. Depending on the lie of the land, extensive courtyards develop vertically or horizontally on the multi-axes. In small dwellings, the courtyards are narrow and the buildings closely connected. The courtyard of the quadrangle serves as the outdoor living space for the family.

Ritual architecture was also based on the quadrangle, albeit a variation. The buildings on all sides are further apart and huge courtyards are formed by square or round walls between them. An altar for sacrificial ceremonies stands in the centre. This basic quadrangular form is to be seen in the ritual architecture of the Han Dynasty and the Temple of Heaven of the Ming and Qing dynasties in Beijing.

The quadrangle layout reached its perfection in the palatial architecture of China, the Forbidden City in Beijing being its most outstanding representative. The public square in front of the Hall of Heavenly Peace, site of the grand state ceremonies held on the lunar New Year's Day or on the ascension to the throne of a new emperor, as well as the east and west six imperial palaces are based on variations of the quadrangle, the only difference being the greater scale and grandeur and the more rigid layout of the buildings.

During the long period of feudalism in China, social and ethical concepts developed whereby the clan became the all-important centre; a closed and concentrated set-up, characterized by a strong sense of the primary and the secondary, the honorable and the humble. The architecture of the country reflected this social arrangement in that various buildings serving different purposes were arranged round a courtyard. As mentioned above, palatial and ritual architecture was based on this concept as was the Chinese Buddhist monastery.

During the Northern and Southern Dynasties, it became the fashion to give up dwellings for monasteries. At that time many Buddhist monasteries were rebuilt on the basis of these houses, and the Buddhist worshipping hall was the former main hall of the dwelling. This kind of Buddhist monastery with the quadrangle as the fundamental unit otherwise gave no external indication of its function and particularities. However, by arranging buildings along the vertical axis and putting the main hall in an eminent position, disciples were initiated in the formalities of religious worship. The Longxing Monastery in Zhengding, Hebei Province, is a typical example, showing the plan layout of Buddhist architecture in China.

The Longxing Monastery First built in the 2nd year of the reign of Kaihuang (586) of the Sui Dynasty, it was initially called the Longcang (dragon-hiding) Monastery, and was moderate in scale. In the early years of the Song Dynasty, it was renamed the Longxing (dragon-rising) Monastery. In the 4th

**Roushen Precious Hall
on Mount Jiuhua**

The hall has double eaves and
a sloping roof. It is reached
by a long, straight flight of
stone steps leading upwards.
Iron chains between stone
pillars flank each side, offering
welcome assistance to visitors
as they climb the 81 steps.
In the hall there is a seven-
storeyed pagoda crowned by a
canopy , and the lowest storey
is enshrined with a statue of the
Dizang King. The entrance right
in the middle is set back and has
a horizontal tablet bearing the
words "The first mountain in the
southeast".

year of the reign of Kaibao (971), Emperor Taizu of the Song Dynasty, it
was greatly expanded and began to take on its present shape. The halls of the
monastery were arranged on an axis measuring 380 m from north to south.
Its southernmost tip ends in a glazed screen wall. To its north are three mono-
arched stone bridges. Straight over the bridge is the temple gate flanked by a pair
of stone lions, and passing through one enters a narrow courtyard with drum
and bell towers on either side. Beyond Dajue Liushi Hall is a paved path flanked
by the east and west chambers. The oldest extant building, Moni Hall, stands
before one. This great hall, built in 1052, is cruciform. Moving in a northerly
direction and passing the Commandment Altar, one suddenly finds oneself
face to face with the magnificent three-storied Dabei Ge (big sorrow pavilion).
Rising to an impressive 33 m, it has a double-eaved sloping roof. This pavilion,
the Jiqing Ge (celebration-gathering pavilion) and the Yushu Ge (imperial-book
pavilion) all stand side by side. To the east and west are the Ghalan and Founder
Halls and directly in front of these buildings and almost as old as the Moni
Pavilion are the scripture-rotation hall and the Cishi Pavilion. All these on the
200 m long and narrow axis in front of the monastery and the beautiful Dabei
Ge, set off as it is by the accompanying minor halls, constitute an architectural
entity of great religious appeal.

The Guangji Monastery　The monastery is located at Xisi in the city of Beijing. Opposite its temple gate is a bustling street, and inside is a broad public square for the parking of cars and the halting of horses. Bell and Drum Towers stand on the east and west sides of the courtyard. The Hall of Heavenly Kings, in which the Four Heavenly Kings (four Lokapalas) are enshrined, stands on its northern side and behind this stands the principal building of the monastery, the Precious Hall of the Great Hero, in which the third generation Buddha is enshrined. Behind this again stands the Yuantong (flexible hall) where Guanyin Bodhisattva is enshrined for worship. To be found in the last courtyard is the Scripture Hall. To the right of the central axis running from south to north, there are also a few subsidiary courtyards where the monks lead their daily lives. The whole monastery is enclosed by side halls and corridors thus forming a quiet and peaceful space shut off from the outside world.

Although the architectural structure of Buddhist monasteries is similar to that of large palaces, they gain their religious atmosphere by the arrangement of the rooms and their fittings. The main building is generally the Precious Hall of the Great Hero, which is customarily located in the third or fourth courtyard on the axis. It is wider than its depth and its plan is rectangular. As Buddhism in China advocates multi-Buddha enthronement and worship, such a plan lends itself to the sacrificial arrangement of the Buddhist statues. The principal Buddha is generally placed on the platform situated in the centre of the rear section of the hall, with either three-generation or seven-generation Buddhas side by side, or one Buddha in the middle flanked by disciples and Bodhisattvas. In front of the Buddha are the incense-burner table and the mat for pilgrims to kneel on and worship. The pillars are often draped with streamers, curtains and umbrellas. Some Buddhist monasteries even have arhat statues set up in front of the gables.

The Foguang Monastery　The Foguang Monastery on Wutai Mountain in Shanxi Province is located north of Doucun Village, 30 km northeast of Wutai County. With its rear part set against the cliff, the monastery faces west onto open country. The elevated position of the Eastern Great Hall allows a panoramic view of the countryside to be had from its front platform. The hall one sees today dates from the 11th year of the reign of Dazhong (857) of the Tang Dynasty, when it was rebuilt following the destruction that took place during the years of persecution by the Tang emperor Wuzong. Covering an area of 677 m^2, the hall is seven bays wide and four bays deep. The platform inside

Foguang Monastery on Mount Wutai

One of the famous monasteries on Mt.Wutai, it was built during the reign of Emperor Xiaowen (471-499) of the Northern Wei Dynasty and was highly popular during the Tang. A three-storeyed Maitreya Hall rising to a height of 32 m and seven-bays wide originally stood on the site of the present-day Eastern Great Hall. The whole monastery was completely destroyed during the persecution of Buddhism under Emperor Wuzong. The Eastern Great Hall was built in the 11th year of the reign of Dazhong (857).

carries a Sakyamuni statue sitting cross-legged in meditation on a rectangular Sumeru throne. In the next bay to the left the principal statue is Maitreya Buddha, each foot placed on a lotus flower, and in the next bay to the right Amitaha sits cross-legged in meditation on a hexagonal Sumeru throne. The outer bays on the left and right house Samantabhadra riding an elephant and Guanyin Bodhisattva on a lion respectively. Sakyamuni is flanked by two senior disciples, Ananda and Kasyapa, as well as two other Bodhisattvas. In front squat two Bodhisattvas offering a sacrifice. The other Buddhist statues also have Bodhisattvas in various postures in front of them, also offering sacrifices. At both ends of the Buddhist platform there are armoured dharma-protecting guardians with sword in hand. Among the many Buddhist statues there is also a female secular figure sitting cross-legged in meditation with her hands tucked deep into her sleeves. This is the woman patron Ning Gongyu, who contributed to and built the great hall. Altogether it houses over 30 Buddhist sculptures,

large and small. Of lively expression and smoothly sculpted, they represent rare works of art from the Tang Dynasty. 296 arhat statues stand on the stone-paved platform in front of the great hall gables. The murals which originally decorated the interior walls no longer exist, only a few traces remaining in the bricked holes of the column heads.

The Eastern Great Hall of the Foguang Monastery consecrates five leading Buddhas. Other Buddhist halls consecrate the past seven Buddhas, the six Buddhas before Sakyamuni (Pibosh Buddha, Shiqi Buddha, Pishefu Buddha, Juliusun Buddha, Junahanmuni Buddha and Kasyapa Buddha), as well as the Sakya Buddha. In the last Hall of the Seven Buddhas in the Baoguo Monastery on Mount Emei, Sichuan Province, these seven Buddhist statues are enshrined in a row.

Even more Buddhist monasteries enshrine in their Precious Hall of the

Great Hero the three Buddhist statues known as the three-generation Buddhas. There are two versions: the three-generation Buddhas representing the past, present and future, also known as the vertical three-generations, whereby the statue in the centre is generally the present-generation Buddha, with the past-generation Kasyapa Buddha and the future-generation Maitreya Buddha on either side, and the so-called horizontal three-generation Buddhas, the one in the centre representing the present shapo world, the ones on either side the Drug Master Buddha of the eastern pure glazed world and Amitabha of the western land of ultimate bliss. An example of the type is to be found in the Precious Hall of the Great Hero in the Xiantong Monastery on Mt. Wutai. From the Tang and Song dynasties onwards, many monasteries began to enshrine tall and voluminous Guanyin indoors. Buddhist halls therefore began to emerge in the form of storeyed buildings. Such architecture of wooden structure, either in design or construction, meant that its builders had to be precise, and the results were often exquisite. Designed purely to house standing statues, the Buddhist statue filled the hall entirely, imbuing it with the spirit of Buddhism.

The Dule Monastery the Guanyin pavilion of the Dule Monastery in Jixian County, Hebei Province, was built in the 2nd year of the reign of Tonghe (984) of the Liao Dynasty (907-1125). Seen from the outside, it is a two-storeyed pavilion, 23 m high, with a single eave and sloping roof. The interior is three-storeyed and in the middle is a clay-sculpted eleven-faced Guanyin, rising to 16 m. The Buddha's face is lit up by the source of light emanating from the skylight above; the rest of the pavilion, however, is kept dim, producing a deeply religious atmosphere. The Thousand-hands and Thousand-eyes Guanyin statue in the Mahayana Hall of the Puning Monastery in Chengde, Hebei Province, soars to a height of 22.8 m. In Wanfu Pavilion of the Lama Temple in Beijing, there is a 18 m high Buddhist statue, sculptured out of a whole piece of white sandalwood. These two pavilions are both masterly examples of the art of high pavilion building in China. In addition to the Precious Hall of the Great Hero, the main Buddhist building, there are also the Hall of Heavenly Kings, the Maitreya Hall, the Drug Master Hall, the Guanyin Hall and the Founder Hall, each with its own design and arrangement according to the religious sect. Generally, these minor halls are not very tall and their different spatial arrangements uncomplicated. Some enshrine and worship the Four Heavenly Kings, dharma-protecting Guardians, Shijanto and others. Others enshrine and worship Maitreya, a very stout monk with a broad smile on his face, his

The Bronze Hall of the Xiantong Monastery, Mt. Wutai

The Bronze Hall of the Xiantong Monastery is 4.7 m wide, 4.5 m deep and 8.3 m high. Viewed from outside, it has two storeys, but inside it has only one. Each of the four sides on the second floor has six dividing screens. A corridor with sloped roofing runs round the whole floor. Each of the four sides on the lower floor has eight dividing sceens. All these dividing screens are movable.

naked breast and belly exposed (also known as the monk with the cloth bag). Still others enshrine and worship the great scholar Guanyin, who watches over, or hears the voices of the suffering and grants whatever is requested, or the founder of a religious sect, who built the first temple on a famous mountain. These halls are either arranged in front of or behind the main hall on the central axis or stand next to each other on either side of the main hall, and in the two chambers of the courtyard. Minor as they are, they are still very important components of the monastery.

To intensify the religious atmosphere, Buddhist halls are often fully painted with coloured drawings on a religious theme. Some even use relief sculpture as decoration, achieving a strong three-dimensional effect. Still other monasteries have hundreds of Buddhist statues arranged in rows from ceiling to floor. The bronze hall of the Xiantong Monastery in Wutai, Shanxi Province is a good example. The inner walls of the partition board are covered on both sides with Buddhist statues. In Tathagata Hall (Ten-thousand Buddhas Tower) of the Zhihua Monastery, the little Buddhist niches on the wall were filled with clay-sculptured Buddhist statues coated with gold powder. Less than four inches high, they are arranged in rows extending to the ceiling.

The monastery included other buildings too: on the ceremonial side, the hall for scripture lectures, the scripture printing house, the Pilu Hall, the scripture tower and the hall for meditation; on the domestic side, buildings such as the abbot's room, the monks' living quarters, the dining hall, the tea-room, the store-house, the kitchen, the so-called life-prolonging hall for senior monks to live out their retirement. These buildings were all located in the wing courtyards, separated from the main halls to avoid disturbance of the solemn religious ceremonies.

Buddhist architecture in China also includes extant buildings that in structure and design are unique. A case in point is the dramatic hanging monastery in Hunyuan County, Shanxi Province. Located in a gorge running through Mt. Hengshan, it has over 30 pavilions and towers literally hanging from the cliff face. Another example again is the Qiaolou (bridge tower) Hall in Jingjing, Hebei Province, which stands on a bridge spanning a deep valley; a truly impressive sight when, during heavy rain, the hall keeps looming up through the mists. Yet another example is the beamless hall consisting purely of brick and stone tubular arches and based on the wooden structures of ancient times. Cases in point are the Linggu Monastery in Nanjing, the Yongzha Monastery in Taiyuan, the Wannian Monastery on Mt. Emei and the Xiantong Monastery on Mt. Wutai.

III. The Characteristics of the Architectural Art of the Lamasery

1. Regional Influence

Lamaseries in China are mainly scattered over Tibet, Inner Mongolia and the provinces of Qinghai, Gansu and Sichuan, and were mostly built during the Ming and Qing dynasties. In structural appearance, lamaseries and monasteries of the Han territory are rather different. In the scattered regions mentioned above, local ethnic customs and architectural style, the weather and the environment, the material available as well as the links with Han territory all played a role.

In Tibet, lamaseries are mostly of block-house style. The traditional three-part treatment consisting of foundation, body and roof practised in Han territory was not applied, and instead, the Tibetans, taking the topography into account erected stone walls directly from the earth's surface. For reasons of insulation, they were thick and solid. Lamaseries have a close-beam wooden structure on top and the roofs are rammed flat with powdery limestone and mostly level. The houses are arranged round a central courtyard with the main Buddhist building being given prominence by the richness of its decoration. The primary colour of the lamasery wall is white and it is perforated by small and narrow openings with frames in the form of a black ladder. The outer walls

of the chief Buddhist halls are painted reddish brown and the governmental offices of the Living Buddha yellow. The eaves are decorated with brown decorative ribbons, made from a kind of white plant peculiar to Tibet. The soft woollen quality of the ribbon contrasts with the rock wall. In some important monasteries, the roofs of the principal Buddhist halls and spiritual pagodas for the deceased resemble a sloping hillside with prominent angles covered with gilded bronze tiles. With their gold-topped stone pillars inscribed with Buddhist scriptures, the green and gold roofs look particularly splendid in the bright sunshine of the plateau. Particularly characteristic of Tibetan architecture is the planned contrast between decoration and colour.

The architecture of the lamasery in Inner Mongolia and Qinghai still retains its Tibetan style in total layout and decoration, but has additional artistic elements of the Han style. The lamasery of Xilamulunzhao of the Ulanchabu grasslands of Inner Mongolia combines elements of the Han and of Tibet. Right in front of the great hall is a two-storeyed protruding pillar corridor. Surrounding the same building is a mono-storeyed pillar corridor and on top of the flat roof is a house-top construction resembling a sloping hillside. The low side wall is sculptured with ornamental designs made brick carvings. This is something Tibetan architecture does not have. On the east side of the great

The Bronze Pagoda of the Xiantong Monastery, Mt.Wutai / opposite left

Only two of the original five bronze pagodas in the Xiantong Monastery still exist, representing the Eastern and Western platforms. The pagoda shown stands on the former. Soaring to a height of 7 m, it has 13 octagonal storeys. The body of the pagoda is richly decorated with exquisitely moulded Buddhist statues and patterns.

Buddhist Statues in the Bronze Hall of the Xiantong Monastery, Mt. Wutai opposite right

More than 10,000 tiny bronze-cast Buddhas completely cover the walls of the Bronze Hall presenting a unique sight. A graceful bronze-cast image of a Manjusri scholar is enshrined in the centre of the lotus seat.

Relief Sculpture in the Shuxiang Monastery, Mt. Wutai / upper

A large relief sculpture extends over three walls in the Manjusri Tower of the Shuxiang Monastery. Presented is the Buddhist world of ancient India in miniature form. 500 arhats are to be seen, each unique, in an abstract, brightly coloured landscape of towering cliffs. The sculpture serves to intensify the religious atmosphere of the place.

Interior View of the Beamless Hall in the Linggu Monastery / lower

In the Linggu Monastery located on the southeast slope of the Zhongshan Mountain in Nanjing, there is a beamless hall. Built of brick and rock, it has a vaulted roof and is an example of the architecture of the Ming Dynasty. Composed of three lengthy archways, the middle one is the largest, the two at both ends having windows.

hall is a quadrangular complex purely in Han style, especially built for the Living Buddha, who came to the Xilituzhao Lamasery in Huhhot for a summer retreat. The Guardian Hall (lesser gold-tiled hall), Greater Scripture Hall, Astronomy Academy, the Lesser Flower Monastery and other buildings in Huangzhong, Qinghai Province, adopted the Han style on a large scale. Typical of this style are, for example, the sloping roofs, the dougong brackets, the glazed tiles, the grey dry brick walls, the square pavilions and the verandas. Organically integrated into the traditional Tibetan architecture, they possess an even richer and more unique style.

During the Qing Dynasty, some lamaseries were also built in Beijing and Hebei Province. The architectural style of these lamaseries was basically Han. The strict symmetric layout on the central axis, the arrangement from the temple gate to the temple buildings are both typical of the Han monastic style. Only in architectural decoration, architectural form and house-top structure can the influence of lamasery architecture be seen. The Puning Monastery of Chengde in Hebei Province was built in 1755. Its front half was built according to Han-style layout, and its rear half was built according to that of the Sangye Monastery in Tibet. The chief temple buildings were all on the central axis. The main hall, the Mahayana tower, was completely of wooden beam structure, but the gable section was given Tibetan blind windows in the form of ladders. Covered with five square tapering tops, the tower was built in the style of Wuce Great Hall in the Sangye Monastery in Tibet.

2. Free-style Layout

The lamaseries in Tibet are not particular about a clear axis line. This is one of the characteristics that differentiates them from Buddhist monasteries of the interior. All buildings in a lamasery are freely arranged around the chief temple buildings such as the Cuoqin Great Hall or the Spiritual Pagoda Hall for eminent monks who had died. The various buildings could be distinguished by the different colours of their outer walls or by the decorative objects they were furnished with. In general, they were large-scale and from a distance gave the impression of a densely populated township, with row upon row of buildings in dazzling colours.

The Zhebang Monastery, one of the three large monasteries in Lhasa and located halfway up Mt. Gengpeiwuci in the western suburbs of the city, covers an area of 200,000 m^2 and is thus the monastery largest in scale in Tibet. Its

The Gold Crown of the Jixiang Faxi Hall in the Xumifushou Monastery

The sloping, double-eaved roof of the Han-style Jixiang Faxi Hall is covered with glittering fish-scale tiles. On top of its main ridge is a tall gold crown representing a dharma bell. The zoomorphic ornaments in the form of grotesque animals placed at either end of the ridge and at the eave corners are Tibetan in style.

name Zhebang, meaning a heap of rice in Tibetan, derives from the fact that the mainly white buildings are scattered all over the mountain slope. Of the four scripture halls, the largest is called Luohanlin Zhacang and together with Guomang Zhacang and Deyang Zhacang, offers facilities for monks to study the theories of the exoteric sect. The domestic buildings are arranged in scores of so-called Kangcun villages, and each village provides accommodation for monks from a particular area; the Mongolian lamas living in Sangluo Kangcun village and the Qinghai lamas in Hamudong Kangcun village etc. The senior lamas have their own administrative office and private residence. The buildings went up successively over a long period and because of this lack of overall planning the architecture varies, offering an interesting mixture of different buildings and layouts.

3. Inner Decoration of Buddhist Buildings and Scripture Halls

Another characteristic of Lamaist architecture in Tibet is the inner decoration of Buddhist buildings and scripture halls. The inner space of Tibetan monasteries is, in contrast to that of Han-style buildings, more generous in every

Interior View of Cuoqin Great Hall in the Zhebang Monastery

Extending over an area of 2,000 m², the Great Hall with its 183 pillars can accommodate 9000 lamas simultaneously chanting the scriptures. A skylight in the centre of the roof allows daylight to penetrate, and brightly-coloured pennants and streamers are draped over the wooden pillars and beams. Row upon row of cushions are spread out over the floor for the lamas.

way, enabling numerous monks to chant the scriptures in chorus. The scripture halls are richly draped with all sorts of streamers and curtains, and the pillars are wrapped in colourful felt blankets. Cushions litter the floor. In the vast scripture hall, only a ray of sunlight is allowed to penetrate via the central protruding skylight, the rest is left in darkness, producing the mystic atmosphere unique to Lamaist architecture. In the big scripture hall of Tiecanglangwa Zhacang (hearing and thinking academy) in the Labuleng Monastery of Xiahe, Gansu Province, the main hall is 11 bays wide (100 m long) and 75 m deep with 140 pillars following on from each other, the length and breadth of the hall. It can hold 4,000 lamas simultaneously chanting the scriptures. The Cuoqin Great Hall in the Labuleng Monastery in Lhasa covers an area of 2,000 m² and has 183 pillars. It is also profusely decorated with streamers and curtains. Early on, each morning, several thousand lamas can be seen sitting row upon row on cushions chanting scriptures, accompanied by drums and trumpets. Tea is later brought in wooden buckets from the kitchen to the scripture hall by young lamas; an impressive sight to those witnessing the scene for the first time.

Some Lamaist monasteries have a specially built hall for the worship of Buddha. The Qiangba Buddhist Hall in the Zhashilunpu Monastery of Xikazi rises to a height of 30 m. Here the 26 m high Qiangba Buddha, known as Maitreya in Han territory, was enshrined and worshipped. To cast the Buddha, 100,000 kg of red copper and 8,900 liang of gold were used, and to provide a better view, a five-storeyed tower was built around the statue, enabling a good view to be had. Buddhist statues in Juekang Hall of the Dazhao Monastery are divided into groups. Right in the middle (east side) is the statue of Sakyamuni, brought into Tibet by Princess Wencheng. On the north and south sides facing each other are the Buddhist statues of Cizun and the Thousand-hands Guanyin. On the west side of the 2nd storey Songzan Gampu, Princess Bhrkuti and Princess Wencheng are enshrined. All four sides of the house-top of Juekang hall have a gold tower, so as to give prominence to the position of these four halls. In front of the Buddhist statue enshrined in the Lamaist monasteries, butter lamps are kept burning day and night. Buddhist followers show their reverence by adding a small piece of the butter they have brought with them to each lamp.

4. Murals

Typical too for the Lamaist monasteries in Tibet are the murals depicting religious themes on the interior walls of the scripture halls and Buddhist buildings. One can still today find their traces in the cave monasteries built during the Wei, Jin, the Northern and Southern dynasties. Murals were also

Murals of the Jubilant Buddha's Warrior Attendants in the Summer Scripture Hall of the Ta'er Monastery

The Ta'er Monastery is a Tibetan Buddhist temple. The bright colours and the lively and detailed figures, each individually portrayed in a standing or sitting position, each with a different bearing, make these murals enchanting examples of the technique.

applied to the interior walls of the many monasteries built between the Tang and Song dynasties, not only intensifying the religious atmosphere in the monastery but also playing an important role in the propagation of Buddhism.

In Tibet, Lamaist mural paintings in the three regions of Shannan, Houzang and Qianzang can be classified into three styles. Common to all is a method of painting adopted from the interior, Nepal and India but nevertheless based on traditional Tibetan painting, as well as the employment of strong contours. An art emerged that exhibited the vigour and emotion of the highland people. The themes included religious narratives, Buddhist stories in a disguised form, the lives of famous figures, historical events, Tibetan landscapes and social customs, the architecture of Buddhist monasteries, religious festival and local legends. The stories, coming to life under the painter's brush, enjoyed great popularity. The basic colour chosen was dark green to achieve a unifying effect and the space covered either by a single story of dramatic content or consecutive narratives. Between these groups of paintings were sections filled with paintings of trees, plants and flowers, coloured clouds, mountains and rivers as well as different patterns. Brilliant examples of the art of the Tibetan mural are to be seen in the thousand-Buddha corridor in the Dazhao Monastery and the Sunshine Hall in Potala Palace.

IV. Decoration, Artistic Creation, etc.

In addition to the principal Buddhist buildings and those in which the monks worshipped Buddha, chanted the scriptures and led their daily lives, there were also others such as the bell and drum tower, the pavilion housing the stone tablet, the memorial archway and perhaps a pavilion on a terrace. Stone animals were an additional adornment as were the gardens. They all played a role in either emphasizing the axis position or symbolizing a monastery's status, even perhaps adding a lighter touch to the otherwise solemn atmosphere of the monastery or an artistic effect to the architecture in general.

The bell and the drum were originally musical instruments used in a Buddhist mass. Beating the drum is a signal for religious services and meals. Inside the temple gate of larger monasteries, bell and drum towers were built on the left and right, symmetric to each other. This symmetric layout effectively gives prominence to the position of the principal halls. The plan of bell and drum towers is generally square. Two storeyed and double-eaved, some are slim,

The Glazed Archway of the Putuozongsheng Monastery

The Putuozongsheng Monastery was built against a mountain. Although it has a free layout with no clear central axis, it can still be divided into three parts, front, middle and rear. This glazed archway in pure Han style is located in the middle and comprises seven towers. The archway is three-bays wide and four pillars deep. The horizontal tablets on the front and on the back are inscribed with the words "Buddhist doctrine is accommodating" and "The Buddhist Statue is Sacred."

graceful and beautifully constructed, others are natural, poised and dignified. There are many extant examples of monasteries with bell and drum towers, such as the Puning Monastery of Chende in Hebei Province, the Fayuan Monastery in Beijing, Pusading on Wutai Mountain, the ancient Longhua Monastery in Shanghai and the Xilituzhao Monastery in Inner Mongolia. The Hanshan (cold mountain) Monastery in Suzhou became world-famous through the poem "Night Anchoring at Fengqiao" by the Tang poet Zhang Ji. The lines, "Outside Gusu City, Cold Mountain Temple...... late at night, the sound of its bell reaches a traveller's boat," are wonderfully lyrical, with a strong appeal even today. Many monasteries have pavilions to house the stone tablet recording when and why the monastery was built and its history. There are two categories of stone tablet, the first granted by imperial decree and particularly finely made. It is placed in

The Stone Archway of Pusading on Mt. Wutai

In the second courtyard of Pusading (Bodhisattva Crown) and facing Manjusri Hall, stands this two-pillared stone archway, engraved with the inscription, "Scenic Beauty of Wutai" by Emperor Kangxi. The two pillars of the archway resemble two "huabiao". The pillars are supported and embraced by drumshaped stone .The pillar cap and the horizontal beam are carved with decorative patterns, giving prominence to the commemorative nature of "huabiao" an ornamental pillar often seen in the grounds of palaces, imperial gardens and mausoleums.

the imperial pavilion especially built to house it and standing in a prime location in the middle of the first courtyard beyond the temple gate. The pavilion's plan is square and it is double-eaved with a glazed top, symbolizing the authority and standing of the monastery. The second category of stone tablet is generally located in a secondary position or placed along a paved path in the open or in a corridor. It is inscribed with poems written both by the local chief executive and a well-known man-of-letters. These tablets may have no direct connection with the monastic architecture, but can serve to intensify the cultural atmosphere of the monastery, or even raise its standing. Some monasteries have stone lions or stone elephants placed on either side of the temple gate. The moulding of these stone objects differs according to when and where it was done, and some have interesting, if sometimes far-fetched, legends associated with them. Other monasteries also have memorial archways either in the courtyard in front of the gate or on the platform in front of the great hall. The point of these edifices, generally made of wood, brick, stone and coloured glaze, was to proclaim different virtues and merits. The glazed archway of the Wuofo (sleeping Buddha) Monastery in Beijing, the wooden archway in the Bishan Monastery on Mt. Wutai are typical examples. Gardens, too, were laid out outside monastery buildings, cases in point being the Jiechuang Monastery in Suzhou and the Dajue and Biyun monasteries in Beijing. Pools, and pavilions on a bridge or terrace behind the monastery or in the garden itself, were characteristic of such resting places for the pilgrims, travelling scholars and Buddhist worshippers coming to the monastery.

The patterns used for decoration were often based on Buddhist symbols; the lotus flower, the diamond pestle, the Heavenly Kings, the guardian statues all being examples. The patterns created, highly decorative and artistic, were applied to ceilings, the stone base of columns, the base of pagodas, banisters and the caisson ceilings of the great halls. Decorative patterns inspired by the local folk-art were also used, and here, the ornaments used in Tibetan Lamaist architecture were unique. Tall gold pillars were erected on the flat roofs of lamaseries and inscribed for instance with Buddhist scriptures, the dharma wheel and gold deer. These pillars are visible from a great distance, the sun often catching the gleaming gold of their surface.

Illustration of the Principal Features of the Chinese Buddhist Pagoda (I)

The Buddhist pagoda originated in India. After being introduced into China and fully integrated into the architectural traditions of the country, many forms were recreated, such as the tower-style pagoda, the pavilion-style pagoda, the diamond-throne pagoda, the dagoda, the flower pagoda, the guojie pagoda (overhead pagoda spanning a lane), the baoqie yinjing pagoda (pagoda enshrining the precious case printed with scriptures) and others. The Chinese Buddhist pagoda did not only provide room for the enshrinement of Buddhist statues but a means of obtaining a bird's-eye view of the surrounding countryside. There are two kinds of tower-style pagodas; the wooden and the brick and stone-paved. Both are typical for China. The pagoda of the Foguang Monastery in Yingxian County, Shanxi Province, is the oldest wooden tower pagoda still in existence. After the Tang Dynasty, the brick and stone-paved

Section of the Sakya Pagoda in the Foguang Monastery (tower-style pagoda)

The Sakya pagoda in the Fogong Monastery is popularly known as the Yingxian wooden pagoda. Built in the 2nd year of the reign of Qingning (1056) of the Liao Dynasty (907-1125), it is the highest wooden Buddhist pagoda still in existence in China . The pagoda is located inside the temple gate in front of the Great Hall on the central axis. Its plan is octagonal. Seen from the outside, it has five storeys with four doublelayers, but actually has nine storeys with six layers of eaves. Built on a two-stepped stone base, the pagoda is 67.3 m high. Structurally, it is a tubular pagoda within another tubular pagoda. Between the column caps are inner lintels and plate lintels, and between the column feet are difu beams and other horizontal structural members. 60 kinds of Dougong bracket were actually used in the pagoda. The combination of column net and structural members resulted in an inner and outer trough system. The inner trough is for enshrining Buddha, the outer trough allows people to ascend and descend.

Elevation of the Renshou Pagoda in the Kaiyuan Monastery (tower-style pagoda)

Popularly known as the West pagoda, the Renshou pagoda is situated west of the Great Hall in the Kaiyuan Monastery in Quanzhou City. It was first built in the 2nd year of the reign of Zhenming (916) of the Liang Dynasty of the Five Dynasties. Initially it was of wood but in the first year of the reign of Shaoding (1228) of the Song Dynasty, it was rebuilt of stone and became a stone pagoda. Rising to a height of 44.06 m, the pagoda has an octagonal Sumeru base. Each corner is strengthened by a round pillar, the base of which taking the form of an inverted alms bowl. Between the pillars are inner lintels. Each storey has a pagoda wall, a winding corridor and the pagoda pillar at the centre. Various dougong brackets are used to combine and support the structural members of the different storeys. The spire, anchored by iron chains attached to each corner of the roof, comprises a base, an inverted alms bowl, a lotus flower, the wheel of law and a flower plate.

version built in the style of the wooden structure gradually became paramount. The spatial treatment of the interior of such pagodas is highly varied. For instance, the Renshou pagoda of the Kaiyuan Monastery in Quanzhou, Fujian Province, is a pagoda containing another pagoda serving as a pillar in the centre. The Yunyan pagoda in Suzhou, Jiangshu Province, is a tubular pagoda containing another tubular pagoda. The Kaiyuan pagoda in Zhengding County, Hebei Province, is a hollow tubular pagoda. Close-eaved pagodas are mostly solid, and cannot be climbed. The Songyue pagoda in Henan Province and the Qixia Sheli Pagoda in Nanjing City are cases in point. The Biyun pagoda in Beijing is a famous extant example of the diamond-throne pagoda. The dagoba is also referred to as the pagoda in the form of an inverted alms bowl. The earliest extant pagoda in China is the white pagoda of the Miaoying Monastery in Beijing.

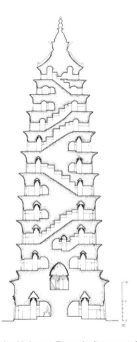

Section of the Yunyan Monastery Pagoda on Huqiu Mountain (tower-style pagoda)

The pagoda of the Yunyan Monastery is also known as the Huqiu pagoda as it is situated on the mountain of the same name. Built in the 6th year of the reign of Xiande (959) of the later Zhou at the latter end of the period of the Five Dynasties, it was a Song pagoda, the oldest, the grandest in scale and the most exquisite in structure. The pagoda is octagonal and has seven storeys. It is built of brick on the lines of a wooden tower and is 47 m high. Each storey has a flat seat, waist beam, inner lintel, dougong brackets, doors and windows. The pagoda not only tapers up gradually storey by storey, but the height of each lessens too. And at the outer-eave of each story corner, a round pillar is set as a support. Right in the middle of each side is a kettle-shaped arch door. On either side of it, the outer wall is divided into three bays with pillars. The central bay is a door, and the two bays on either side latticed windows.

Section of the Kaiyuan Pagoda (tower style pagoda)

The pagoda is located inside the southern gate of Zhengding County, Hebei Province. When it was first built, there was fighting taking place between the Liao and Song dynasties. As the battles were frequent, and the pagoda was high, people would climb up the pagoda and observe the movements of the Liao's army. Hence, the name " pagoda anticipating enemy movements". A brick pagoda in tower-style, it is octagonal and has 11 storeys with an overall height of 84 m. The first storey is rather high, and has a pagoda eave and flat seat. The storeys above have only the pagoda eave but no flat seat. The pagoda eave is paved with bricks layer upon layer so that it is partly suspended in the air. The four front parts have doors, the remaining four sides decorated with blind windows, carved out of brick and taking the form of latticed windows. Sitting on top of the pagoda is an inverted alms bowl decorated with honeysuckle motifs and above this are an iron dew catcher and a bronze pagoda spire.

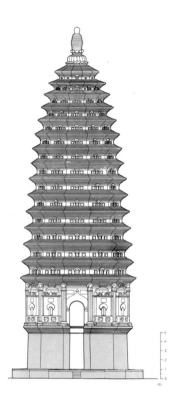

Elevation of the Songyue Pagoda (close-eaved pagoda)

Located at the southern foot of Mt. Songshan about 6 km northwest of Dengfeng County, Henan Province, the Songyue pagoda was built in the 4th year of the reign of Zhengguang (523) of the Northern Wei Dynasty. It is the earliest close-eaved brick pagoda still in existence in China. The pagoda has a tubular structure and brick wall and can be ranked as one of the supreme examples of Chinese architecture.

The whole pagoda is composed of three parts: the pagoda body, the eaves and the crown. The pagoda , set on a low and simple base, has 15 storeys each with eaves built by piling up bricks one of top of the other. The spire, also composed of brick and rocks, has a base in the shape of an inverted alms bowl, a girdle and a ring in the form of upturned lotus flowers. The whole is topped by a seven-storeyed wheel of law and a precious pearl.

Southern Elevation of the Sheli Pagoda in the Qixia Monastery (closed-eaved pagoda)

Located on Mt. Qixia, 17 km northeast of Nanjing, the Sheli pagoda in the Qinxia Monastery is a relic of the Tang Dynasty. It represents one of the oldest stone pagodas south of the Yangtse River. About 15 m high, it takes the form of a small octagonal stone pagoda of five storeys. Its overall composition created a new style of close-eaved pagoda in China. The base has horizontally laid stone pillars round it and is surmounted first by a ring of upturned lotus flowers, then by the Sumeru throne and finally by another broader ring of lotus flowers. The first storey is high, the ones above each with close eaves, between which are small niches decorated with Buddhist statues. The crown, originally a metal spire, was rebuilt and consists of several layers of stone-carved lotus flowers. Built in the style of a wooden pagoda with storeyed eaves, this close-eaved brick pagoda is an architectural gem .

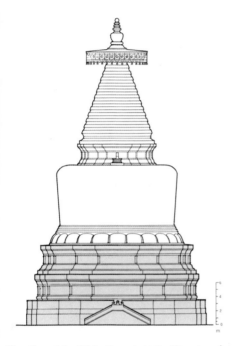

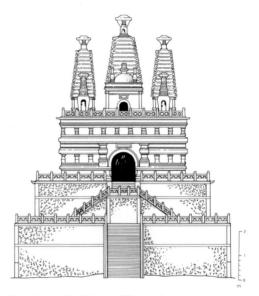

Elevation of the White Pagoda in the Miaoying Monastery (dagoba)

The Miaoying Monastery is situated inside the Fuchengmen Gate in Beijing. It was first built in the 2nd year of the reign of Shouchang of the Liao Dynasty, but in the 8th year of the reign of Zhiyuan (1271), Emperor Shizu of the Yuan Dynasty, the old pagoda was destroyed and a new one built. Due to the white colour of the dagoba, it is known as the White Pagoda and represents a variation of a primitive form of stupa.

The dagoba is composed of three large parts; the base of the Sumeru throne, the pagoda body in the form of an upturned alms bowl and the truncated tapering columns bearing the sign of the Buddhist wheel, known as the 'thirteen days.' The top of the pagoda takes the form of a bronze canopy, topped by a miniature bronze dagoba.

Elevation of the Diamond Throne Pagoda in the Purple Cloud Monastery (Diamond Throne Pagoda)

Located at the eastern foot of the Fragrant Hills in the western suburb of Beijing, the Diamond Throne pagoda behind the Purple Cloud Monastery was built in the 13th year of the reign of Qianlong (1748) of the Qing Dynasty.

Its structure basically followed the Indian design with some Chinese modifications. Of all-white marble, the pagoda is 34.7 m high and has stone stairs leading up to the pagoda seat. The base has two flights of stairs and on top are three landings. The pagoda body has layer upon layer of niches decorated with exquisitely carved Buddhist statues. Right in the middle of the pagoda seat there is an arched opening and on top of the pagoda seat are five close-eaved pagodas 13 storeys high, two dagobas and a small diamond-throne pagoda. The outline of the pagoda is highly decorative with the eight pagoda tips projecting into the sky at different levels. The relief sculptures on the walls of the buildings, portraying Buddhist themes, are an additional adornment.

A Comparison of the Different Plans of Chinese Buddhist Pagodas

There are still over a thousand old pagodas in existence. More common are the square, hexagonal and octagonal in plan , but round and twelve-sided examples can also be seen, if rarely. As far as the design is concerned, there are the tower-style and the close-eaved pagodas as well as the dagoba and diamond-throne pagoda. From the material point of view they can be built of wood, brick or stone. Many changes have taken place in the course of time. The pagoda was originally round, but became square when it became fashionable to build in the style of wooden structures. The pagodas of the Northern and Southern Dynasties, for example, as well as those of the Tang Dynasty were mostly square. Octagonal ones became very rare during the latter dynasty, but began to be built after the period of the Five Dynasties. Occasionally there were hexagonal pagodas, but square ones were very few. In the Song dynasty, octagonal pagodas were on the increase and became the standard type of Buddhist pagoda in this period, continuing to be built up to the Ming and Qing dynasties.

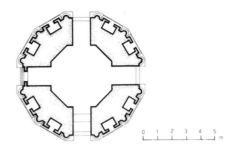

The Songyue Monastery Pagoda in Dengfeng County, Henan

Twelve-angled in paln, wth gates installed on the eastern, western, southern and northern sides, the interior of the pagoda becomes octagonal in plan from the second storey upwards. The building falls into the category of the tubular-style pagoda with close eaves.

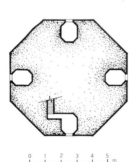

The Youguo Monastery Pagoda in Kaifeng, Henan

Its plan is octagonal, with the stairs going up from the northern gate. The other three gated take the form of small octagonal rooms of unequal sides and without stairs.

The Jueshan Monastery Pagoda in Lingqiu County, Shanxi

The pagoda body and inner rooms are octagonal. In the centre stands a column with dougong brackets of brick supporting the close eaves and the soaring pagoda spire. The pagoda has a two-storeyed base and a Sumeru throne.

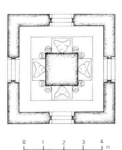

The Four-Gated Pagoda of the Shengtong Monastery in Licheng County, Shandong

Square in plan, it is a single-storeyed stone pagoda with gates on all four sides. A square stone column, fully carved with Buddhist statues, stands in the centre.

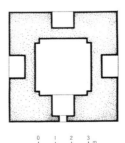

The Xiangji Monastery Pagoda in Xi'an City, Shanxi

The pagoda is square in plan. Built of the usual brick, it has an arched niche on the eastern, western and northern sides. The south side has a gate followed by a square room.

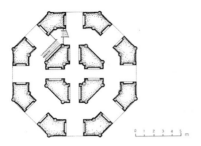

The Yuanyan Monastery Pagoda on Huqiu Mountain near Suzhou, Jiangsu

A brick pagoda built in the style of a wooden structure, it is octagonal in plan with seven storeys, each with waist eaves. The inner design of the pagoda is of tubular structure with a wingding corridor.

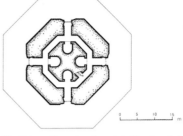

The Kaiyuan Monastery Pagoda in Dingxian, Hebei

Octagonal in plan, the pagoda has 1 storeys each geiven projecting eaves. The pagoda's inner structure is tubular with a winding corridor. Gates are installed on four sides. In the centre is an octagonal column with stairs to enable a commanding view to be had from the top.

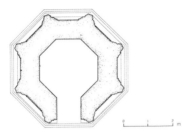

Chan Master Jingzang's Tomb Pagoda in Kaifeng, Henan

A one-storeyed brick pagoda with double eaves, its plan and inner room are octagonal. The front of the pagoda body has been given an arch gate. The even corners of the pagoda body are designed with supporting pillars on the wall.

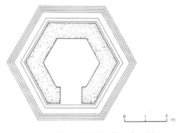

The Founder Pagoda in the Foguang Monastery, Wutai, Shanxi

A double-storeyed pagoda, its plan is hexagonal. The front gate of the elaborately moulded pagoda has a flame-shape design.

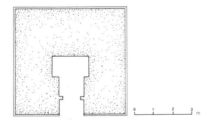

Master Xuan Zhuang's Tomb Pagoda in the Xingjiao Monastery of Xi'an, Shanxi

A solid brick pagoda, its plan is square. The south side of the first storey has been given an arch gate, inside, a square room enshrined with the statue of Xuan Zhuang.

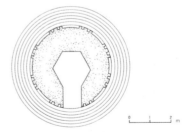

Chan Master Fanzhou's Pagoda, Yuncheng, Shanxi

A round pagoda with a single storey, its base is tubular. The interior of the pagoda body is hexagonal. The pagoda room is empty, and a gate installed on the south front. The room has a caisson ceiling.

Sketch of Grotto Plan and Comparison with Cave Style Evolution

A grotto is a form of Buddhist architecture hollowed out of a cliff face. The procedure originated in India and spread to China during the Northern and Southern Dynasties. It later became fashionable throughout China. At the time the most important grottoes were the Yungang grottoes in Datong, Shanxi Province, the Longmen grottoes in Luoyang, Henan Province, the Tianlongshan grottoes in Taiyuan, Shanxi Province as well as the Mogao grottoes in Dunhuang, Gansu Province, the Maijishan grottoes in Tianshui, Gansu Province and others.

Breathtaking in scale, the Yungang grottoes can be classified into the following types: (1) oval in shape, the cave top forms an arched roof, such as grottoes 5, 16-20; (2) somewhat square in shape with a central pillar and flat ceiling, such as grottoes 1, 2, 6, 11 (3), divided into front and rear chambers. The front wall of the front chamber is hollowed out to form a grotto three bays wide, such as grottoes 9, 10, 12. The Longmen grottoes have altogether over 2,100 caves, big and small. The representative ones are the Guyang cave (arched roof with a wide and deep proportion of 1:2. Sculptured niches line the walls), the Fengxiansi caves, the Wanfo Caves, the Three Binyang Caves (typical grotto of the Northern Wei, its plan is rectangular with two round corners at the rear wall), as well as the Qianxisi Cave. The Tianlongshan grottoes have altogether 21 caves, scattered about in the Western and the Eastern Hills, thirteen in the former, eight in the latter.

The Yungang Grottoes in Datong, Shanxi

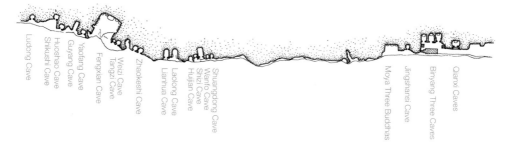

Western Hills of the Longmen grottoes in Luoyang, Henan

Western Hill

Eastern Hill

Tianlongshan Grottoes in Taiyuan, Shanxi

Evolution of the Grotto Type in the Mogao Grottoes of Dunhuang

Also known as the Cave of the Thousand Buddhas, the Mogao grottoes are located 25 kilometres southeast of Dunhuang City in Gansu Province. The steep cliff on the lower eastern slopes of Mt. Mingsha is honeycombed with caves. There are five storeys stretching 1600 m in a south-north direction. Legend has it that the caves were first excavated in the 2nd year of the reign of Jianyuan of the former Qin Dynasty, and through the Northern Wei, Western Wei, Northern Zhou, Sui, Tang and Five dynasties, Song, Western Xia, Yuan and more than ten other dynasties. As these grottoes were excavated over a long period, their design was infinitely varied. Some were in the form of a square Buddhist hall or upturned dou measure. During the process of evolution, those of the Sui Dynasty were more or less the same as those of the Northern Dynasty, and most had a central column. Some , however, had a Buddhist throne instead of the central column. Most Tang Dynasty grottoes no longer used the central column. In the early years of the dynasty, it became the fashion to excavate a front and rear chamber, the front one for various activities, the rear chamber for enshrining and worshipping Buddhist statues. Once the age of prosperity of the Tang was over, the rear chamber became the great hall with a single throne, and only the rear walls had niches for Buddhist statues, thus getting closer to ordinary Buddhist monasteries in plan.

Grotto 371(Early tang period)
Grotto top in the form of sloped roofing

Section

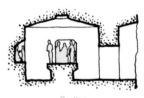

Plan

Grotto 156 (Tang period of prosperity)
Square Grotto in the form of an upturned dou measure

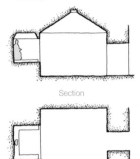

Section

Plan

Grotto 251 (Wei)
Grotto top in the form of sloped roofing

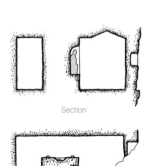

Section

Plan

Grottoe 130 (Flourishing Tang)
Grotto top in the form of an upturned dou measure

Section

Plan

Grotto 305 (Sui)
Square Grotto with upturned dou measure

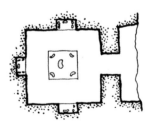

Section

Plan

Plan, Elevation and Section of Tianlongshan Grotto 16

Located halfway up the slopes of Mt. Tianlong, 40 km southwest of Taiyuan in Shanxi Province, the Tianlongshan grottoes have altogether 21 caves scattered over the tops of the Eastern and Western Hills. Eight are on the Eastern Hill, 13 on the Western Hill. The earliest three caves were excavated during the Northern Qi Dynasty (550-577), the rest during the Sui and Tang dynasties.

Tianlongshan grotto 16 was completed in 560. The front corridor is three bays wide, and its octagonal columns are erected on top of a stone column base carved with lotus flower petals. The column is tall and slender, tapering upwards. The proportions of Bolu bracket, inner lintel and the dougong brackets on the lintel, as well as the arched cave-top are all harmonious. The same applies to the height and width of the corridor as well as the ratio between the corridor and the cave door behind. The grotto is a good example of the high degree of perfection the Chinese version of such caves had reached by this time.

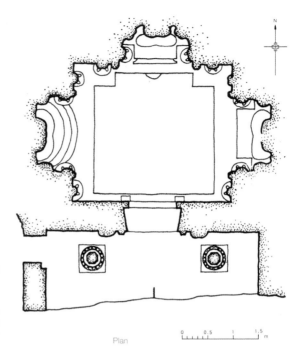

Plan

Elevation

Section

Imaginary Sketch of the Original State of the 4th Maijishan Grotto

Grand in scale, the Maijishan grotto is one of the four famous grottoes in China. Excavated on native architectural lines, the cave is square in shape with flat roofing and a front wall flanked by niches. The most typical cave style is represented by grotto 4 (known as the Tower of Seven Buddhas), located on top of the eastern cliff, its chief characteristic being the colonnades carved in the style of a wooden structure and located outside the Buddhist niche. From the outside, it thus has the appearance of a Buddhist building.

Maijishan grotto 4 is 31.7 m wide, 13 m deep and 15 m high. It has a hall top with a single eave. Both ends of the central ridge have been given zoomorphic ornaments. The front part of the cave has a corridor seven bays wide, in front of which are eight hexagonal stone columns. On top of these are Bolu brackets supporting the eave lintel. Beam ends protrude from the Bolu brackets. The column base takes the form of upturned lotus flower petals. The rear part of the cave has a row of seven Buddhist niches, square in plan, the tops given four sloping roofs, the centres of which are decorated with a lotus flower, magnificent in scale. The whole thus faithfully reproduces a wooden-structured building.

Section

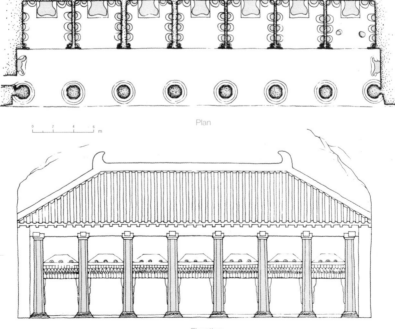

Plan

Elevation

The Excellence of Ancient Chinese Architecture

Buddhist Buildings

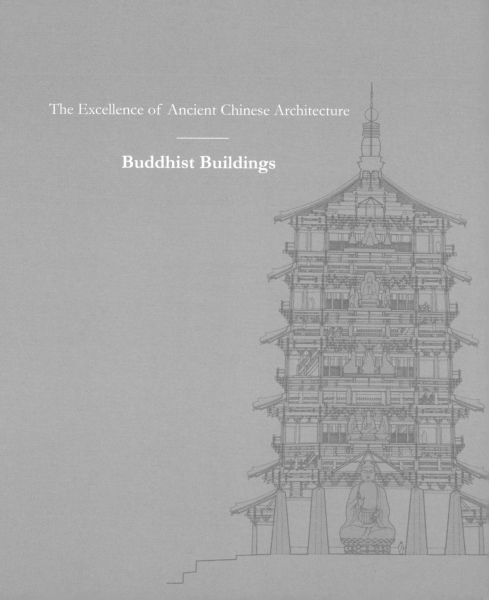

Notes on the Photographs

Buddhist Monasteries, Pagodas and Stone Caves

From the end of the Han Dynasty onwards, Buddhism took root in China, spreading and developing over a period of more than 1,000 years. The original teachings from India became imbued with native Chinese thought on heaven and man; a foreign religion, therefore, with Chinese modifications. As far as its architecture was concerned, it gradually integrated with that of China, in style hardly differing from that stipulated by central government law. In addition to the wooden or brick and stone temple gate, the main hall and other Buddhist buildings, the Buddhist pagoda or tomb pagoda often took on various forms in the monasteries. Unique forms, including those to be found in the stone cave and the lamasery, are also to be seen, chiefly in Northern China and the western localities. To facilitate identification, the monasteries and their location in what is a vast land have roughly been arranged into three regions: Northern China, Central China and the Western Localities. Not only is their appearance described but the reader is also given an insight into their internal structure, their fittings as well as the exquisitely sculptured statues, all an expression of the dignified beauty of Buddhist architecture.

The Temple Gate of the Putuozongsheng Monastery, Chengde, Hebei

After Buddhism spread into China, temples were not only to be seen in abundance in the cities, but in mountainousand forestal regions too. The outer gate was called "shan men," (temple gate) or "san men" (three gate), meaning "gate freeing thrice." The temple gate of the Putuozongsheng Monastery faces south and in front stands a pair of lionson the left and right. Partly crenellated walls extend from its east and west sides, then turn northwards, enclosing the whole monastery. The whole is given a palatial effect by the fact that the temple gate is built in the form of a gate tower with a stone block as base, accessed by three archways, and a palatial-style building on top, five bays wide and one bay deep. Its roof is single-eave and covered with yellow glazed tiles, a green border running along the edge and the ridges. Enshrined in the temple gate are the Four-faced, the Zhangulupeng and the big Black Heaven Mahagala guardians of dharma.

Buddhist Niches in the Dahong Platform, Putuozongsheng Monastery, Chengde, Hebei / opposite page

Located to the rear of the monastery on the highest terrain, the Dahong platform represents the principal building in the Putuozongsheng Monastery. Horizontally, it is divided into three parts: the Red Palace, White Palace and Zhaxia, all built structurally along the lines of Potala Palace in Tibet. The Dahong platform, right in the middle, is 25 m high and built on an 18 m high white base. Seen from the exterior, the platform has seven storeys of windows positioned one above the other to resemble a ladder. The lower four storeys of windows are blind with a solid base. The upper three storeys have windows letting light in alternatively. Running shaft-like from top to bottom, in the middle are glazed niches in yellow and green housing statues of Buddha, a feature that gives prominence to the central axis of the Dahong Platform. Niches containing such figures are to be seen, too, under the low parapet along the edge of the roof on the outer side of the platform, superimposed by drainage spouts jutting out for almost one metre. Extending over an area of approximately 10,000 m^2, the Dahong platform overwhelms by its very magnitude.

Five Pagoda Gate and Stone Elephant in Putuozongsheng Monastery, Chengde, Hebei

The Five Pagoda Gate is located north of the Tablet Pavilion. Large, impressively sculptured stone elephants stand in the front right and left corners of the platform in front of the gate, which is accessed by three arches. The name of the gate originates from the fact that five dagobas stand on the roof, an architectural style that first appeared during the Yuan Dynasty when Lamaism became popular. The pagodas in the monastery and those on the pagoda gate are therefore all in the shape of 'stupa,' composed of three parts: the pagoda base, body and crown. Five kinds of Buddhas are represented, depending on the colour and decoration of each pagoda. The stone elephants represent the Buddhist Mahayana sect. Mighty as the animals are , they symbolize the hard task the Sect has set itself of relieving all creatures from their suffering. With a height of 2.45 m, they are the tallest stone elephants in Chengde.

Tablet Pavilion in the Putuozongsheng Monastery, Chengde, Hebei

Located on the central axis inside the temple gate, the tablet pavilion is a stern-looking Han-style building, square in plan. The pavilion roof is covered with glazed tiles and has double-eaved sloped roofing. Its walls are red with arched entrances on each side. The pavilion sits on a Sumeru throne of white stone surrounded by an ornate marble balustrade. Inside are three square stone tablets standing upright side by side. The tablet in the centre tells of the origin of the monastery, the one on the left the alliance pledged by the Turgut people and the one on the right the history of the Turgut Mongolians. Engraved in Manchurian, Chinese, Mongolian and Tibetan, the tablets represent a precious historical record.

The Glazed Archway in the Putuozongsheng Monastery, Chengde, Hebei

To the north of the Five Pagoda Gate is a pure Han glazed archway, three-bays wide and four columns deep with seven towers. It is similar to both the archway of Sumeru Spring in the Little Western Heaven and that of Jingyi Yuan of the Western Hills in Beijing. Inscribed on the horizontal tablet over the central arch are the words, "Pu Men Ying Xian," meaning the gate delivering all living creatures from their suffering. Here one can see Bodhisattva Guanyin, and the inscription on the board to the rear, "Peng Jie Zhuang Yan," indicates that this is the place where Bodhisattva performed Buddhist rites to save the souls of the dead. The platform in front of the archway has a low wall and flights of steps leading up to it from the front and two sides. Below it, to the left and right, stand two powerful-looking stone lions.

General View of the Putuozongsheng Monastery, Chengde, Hebei

In Tibetan, the free translation of "Putuozongsheng" is Potala, meaning Mount Putuo. There were apparently two places where Bodhisattva performed Buddhist rites to save all living creatures from torment. One was in Lhasa, the other in Zhejiang Province. The monastery of Putuozongsheng was built in the 32nd year of the reign of Emperor Qianlong (1767) of the Qing Dynasty on the same lines as Potala Palace in Tibet. Known as the 'miniature Potala,' it served as the temporary residence of the Dalai Lama. The building complex begins at the foot of the mountain and spreads up to the summit, on which the principal building, the majestic Dahong platform, was set. The technique of arranging the blockhouses of the white platform to follow the vicissitudes of the mountain ridge makes the main building on the summit stand out even more. Reversely, architecture is used to reflect the local physical features—a characteristic of Tibetan monasteries. By integrating traditional Han architecture into the building complex one has before one a unified whole consisting of buildings of great diversity.

Miaogao Zhuangyan Hall on the Dahong Platform of the Xumifushou Monastery, Chengde, Hebei

Miaogao Zhuangyan Hall was the place where Panchen VI gave a lecture on sutra when he stayed at Chengde. It was also built on the Dahong platform. Around it are three-storeyed buildings and between the hall and these buildings there is small yard to let in daylight. The hall has three storeys and it is square in plan with each side containing seven bays. The five bays in the middle are equally wide, the end ones half as wide. The first and second storeys have front corridors. The third storey, with the exception of the three bays in the middle, has an enclosing corridor on the northern side. The three central bays extend from the first to the third storey, the second and third storeys taking the form of a winding corridor with stairs located in the end east and west bays. Buddha Sakyamuni and Zong Khaba, founder of the Lamaist Yellow Sect, are enshrined in the centre of the hall. A throne dating from when Panchen VI delivered his lecture on sutra is installed on the eastern side. Sakyamuni and his two disciples, Ananda and Kasyapa are enshrined on the second storey and on the third were the three Buddhas of the Tantric Sect, but today no longer exist.

Dahong Platform in the Xumifushou Monastery, Chengde, Hebei

The Dahong platform represents the principal building of the Xumifushou Monastery. Its front walls dark red, the building has three rows of evenly placed windows, each row containing 13. The centre of the bottom one, however, is taken up by a door approached by two flights of steps and therefore only has 12. Above the lintel of each window is an ornate relief, superimposed in turn by a beautifully designed canopy. The Dahong platform consists of Miaogao Zhuangyan Hall and a group of buildings surrounding it, forming a square within a square with an intimate inner courtyard. Here there is a feeling of being completely cut off from the outside world. The roofs of the two groups are flat with a low stone parapet, offering a detailed view of the glazed roof of Miaogao Zhuangyan. Pavilions, in the form of a single-eaved palace building, mark each of the four corners of the flat roofs.

Glazed Wanshou Pagoda in Xumifushou Monastery, Chengde, Hebei
opposite page

Situated on top of the mountain behind Wanfazongyuan Hall, the glazed Wanshou Pagoda stands in the rear section of the Xumifushou Monastery. Built on a square white platform, its lower part is composed of an octagonal Sumeru base paved with white stone. The base has balustrades leading round it and a small staircase on the south-facing side. Octagon in shape, the pagoda's walls are decorated with green glazed brick. Each side has a Buddhist niche and the corners are marked by a slender wall-pillar. The pagoda has seven storeys and its lower section was given an octagonal stone base complete with carved stone balustrades from which drip-boards hang. Below this is a spacious winding corridor of wood with a roof of yellow glazed tiles and a green border. It is a simple yet elegant pagoda, the artistry of which is wonderfully impressive. It was originally flanked by two white rectangular terraces but only the remains can now be glimpsed.

Buddhist Statue over the Archway of the Glazed Wanshou Pagoda in Xumifushou Monastery, Chengde, Hebei

An octagonal pillar was placed right in the centre of the Sumeru base of the glazed Wanshou pagoda. A supporting stone wall encircles the first storey and stone archways outside the pagoda connect with the central pillar. These four archways, facing east, west, south and north are decorated with sculptured Buddhist statues, each superimposed by a canopy. The walls of the archways are richly sculpted with winding-plant, mountain, rolling wave and cloud motifs. The picture shows the statue of the Dari Tathagata Buddha.

Jixiang Faxi Hall in the Xumifushou Monastery, Chengde, Hebei / left

Also known as the "Residential Tower," Jixiang Faxi Hall served as the residence of Panchen VI in Chengde. It is a two-storyed building, fivebays wide and three bays deep, with a splendid roof of fine gold tiles the shape of fish scales. The gables boast small Tibetan-style windows, and staircases in the two end bays under the front eave lead up to the second storey. In front of the hall is a small yard enclosed by a group of houses, a feature typical of Tibetan Lamaist architecture. A horizontal board inscribed by Emperor Qianlong hangs in the hall's central bay. Enshrined in the Buddhist hall below is the Sakyamuni Buddha. The guest house and the Panchen's sleeping quarters are located in the east and west end bays, and on the second storey is the hall for Buddhist ceremonies. Religious services were held when the Panchen was in residence and Mongolian princes and dukes came to pay him their respects.

The Gold Crown of the Miaogao Zhuangyan Hall in the Xumifushou Monastery, Chengde, Hebei / right

It was in Miaogao Zhuangyan Hall that Panchen VI delivered his lecture on sutra on the occasion of Emperor Qianlong's birthday, State Master Zhang Jie acting as interpreter. The Scripture Hall was set up there and Khampo Lama sent to teach from Tibet. Like Wanfaguiyi Hall in the Putuozongsheng Monastery, the hall is three storeys high, double-eaved with a tapering top and roofed with bronze tiles, fish-scale in shape. Two dragons ready to pounce decorate each end of the four ridges, the ones above facing the crown, their claws firmly grasping the tiles. The lower four face outwards. Each weighing more than a ton, the bronze sculptures impress by their dramatic pose and make the roofscape truly majestic.

Overall View of the Xumifushou Monastery, Chengde, Hebei

In the 45th year of the reign of Qianlong (1780) of the Qing Dynasty, the Panchen Lama VI made the long and arduous journey to Chengde to congratulate the emperor on his 70th birthday. In order to be able to receive such a high-ranking political and religious leader from Tibet, the Xumifushou Monastery was built along the same lines as the Zhashilunpu Monastery, the Panchen's residence in Xikazi. Located east of the Putuozongsheng Monastery, it covers an area of 37,900 m^2. The overall layout has a central axis, but the buildings are not strictly symmetric. The temple gate, tablet pavilion, glazed archway and Dahong Platform are located in the middle part, with the glazed Wanshou pagoda bringing the whole to a close. Like the outer eight monasteries in Chengde, Xumifushou Monastery also combines the architectural styles of the Han and Tibet.

Mahayana Tower of the Puning Monastery, Chengde, Hebei

One of the eight outer monasteries in Chengde, the Puning Monastery was built in the 20th year of the reign of Qianlong (1775) of the Qing Dynasty. The monastery was given the name of Puning, meaning general peace, both to commemorate the victory over the Zhun'ger tribe and in the hope that a period of peace would follow. A tablet recording the history of the monastery was inscribed and hung up. Mahayana Tower is the principal building in the rear half of the monastery. With a height of more than 36 m, it is seven bays wide and five bays deep. A three-storeyed structure, it has six rows of eaves one on the top of the other. A wooden statue of Guanyin (the Goddess of Mercy), at 24.12 m the largest of its kind in China, stands in the tower. Three storeys of corridors, linked by staircases, run round the statue allowing visitors to admire it from various heights. The inner walls of the tower are decorated with Buddhist niches holding more than 10,000 clay statues gilded with fine gold- a solemn and impressive sight.

Lateral View of Mahayana Tower in the Puning Monastery, Chengde, Hebei

Mahayana Tower was built along the lines of Wuce Great Hall in the Sangye Monastery in Tibet. The building is 36.65 m high and with the exception of the glazed eaves and their ornaments is a purely wooden structure. Viewed laterally, the tower has six storeys and represents the only well-preserved example of a Buddhist monastery with mainly Chinese architectural features, with the different curved roofs harmoniously executed and the glazed tiles, dougong brackets and other wooden structures all typical examples of the Chinese art of building. It does, however, contain certain elements of Tibetan architecture, namely the red wall, to be seen here, with its white ladder-like blind windows.

Elevation and Section of the Mahayana Pavilion in Puning Monastery, Chengde, Hebei

Located northeast of the "Mountain Hamlet for Escaping the Heat" in Chaengde, Hebei Province, the Puning Monastery faces south. It was first built in the 20th year of the reign of Emperor Qianlong of the Qing Dynasty. The layout of the monastery is on a central axis running from south to north. All the main buildings lie on this, resulting in a deep symmetric layout. The Mahayana Pavilion stands at the centre of the terrace, accessed from the front by three flights of south-facing steps. A single flight, with a balustrade composed of typically Qing-style columns allows access from the east and west. The pavilion was designed from the front as a five-storeyed tower with six eaves. The fact that on the third storey the outer bays have only half the width of the other five results in a tapering effect. This is continued on the fourth storey which is only five bays across and three bays deep. At each of its four corners is a yellow pyramid of glazed tiles. The pavilion is an excellent example of the artistic arrangement of roofs in the wooden buildings of the Han.

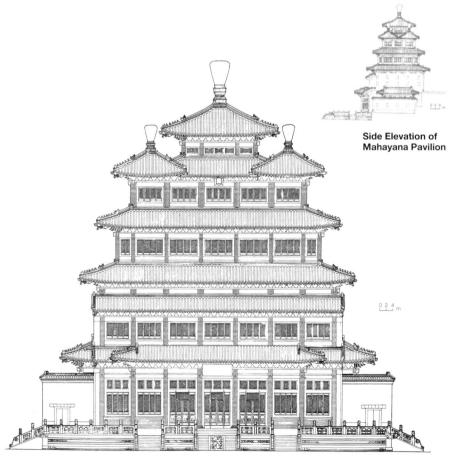

Side Elevation of Mahayana Pavilion

Front Elevation of Mahayana Pavilion

Principal Hall of Mahayana Pavilion of the Puning Monastery

The Mahayana Pavilion is about 37 m high. Seen from the south, it is a five-storeyed tower with six layers of eaves. Seen from the north, it only has four storeys due to the lie of the land. The interior only has three storeys and the rear eave has double layers. The central interior area is five bays wide and three bays deep, cutting through all three storeys to accommodate the approximately 22 m high statue of 'Guanyin with the thousand hands and thousand eyes' carved out of pine, cypress, elm, Chinese fir and native linden wood. It is flanked by wooden statues of Shancai and Longnu. The walls have wooden grottoes, each housing a small clay-sculpted Buddha.

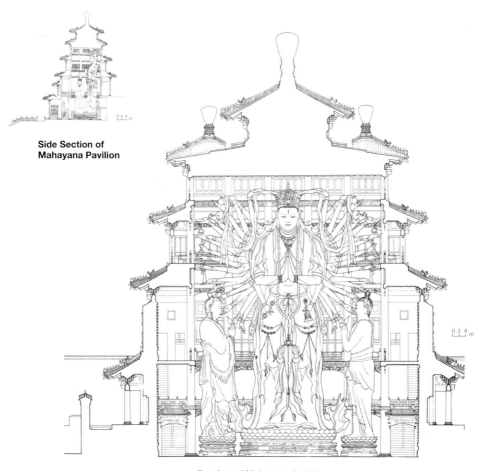

Side Section of Mahayana Pavilion

Section of Mahayana Pavilion

113

Stupa in the City of the Buddhist Monk in the Pule Monastery, Chengde, Hebei

The City of the Buddhist Monk is three storeys high. Each of the four sides of the first storey is provided with an entrance, the main one facing west. The second storey, set back to form a stone platform, is 8 m high and in a crenellated wall. Eight stupas of different colours stand at the four corners and at the centre of each side of the above-mentioned platform; the four stupas at the corners being white, the one due south yellow, the one due north blue, the one due west purple and the one due east black. The eight stupas represent the eight charitable and pious deeds of Sakyamuni: the birth of Buddha, attaining the way, turning the Buddhist Wheel of the Law, showing remarkable ability, descending to the world from the peak of Mount Sumeru, helping and persuading living creatures, thinking endlessly and attaining nirvana. The bodies of the eight stupas are the same in shape, but the Sumeru thrones differ, being square, hexagonal and octagonal.

The Red Pagoda in the Puning Monastery, Chengde, Hebei / opposite page

The great hall of the Sangye Monastery did not only serve as the prototype for the Mahayana Tower but also for the buildings accompanying it. Just as there are four stupas in red, green, black and white in the vicinity of the Sangye Monastery's great hall, Mahayana Tower also has four, albeit smaller in scale and of different shape. Each stupa comprises three parts: the pagoda base, the body itself and the Wheel of the Law. Shaped like a treasure-bottle, the stupas are the same in size, and the body is divided into an upper and lower part, but their colours differ. The whole is topped by the thirteen circles of the Buddhist Wheel of the Law superimposed by the treasure canopy, upturned boat, pearls of the sun and the moon, etc. Shown here is the red stupa next to the Mahayana Tower. Lotus flowers decorate the top of the stupa, symbolizing the place where Buddha was born.

The City of the Buddhist Monk in the Pule Monastery, Chengde, Hebei

One of the eight outer monasteries, the Pule Monastery is situated on the tableland east of the Summer Resort in Chengde. Built in the 31st year of the reign of Emperor Qianlong (1766), the monastery was meant to provide a suitable environment for a submitted ethnic people to have an audience with the sovereign and put their demands forward respectfully and solemnly without seeming disloyal. It is divided into a front and rear part. The former has the traditional layout of a Chinese-style monastery, the latter is taken up by the so-called "tall city of the Buddhist monk," also known as the scripture altar. It is the place for performing Buddhist Tantric dharma of Tibetan Buddhism. The lower part of the altar consists of a three-storied square terrace paved with rectangular stone slabs. Set in the middle of the third storey is the Xuguang Pavilion, the principal building in the rear half of the Pule Monastery. It is circular with double eaves and a tapering top. Externally, it resembles the Temple of Heaven in Beijing.

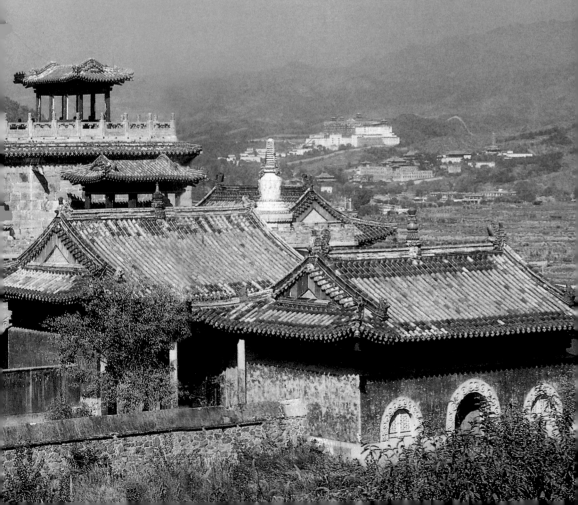

The Precious Hall of the Great Hero in the Tanzhe Temple, Beijing

The Tanzhe Temple is situated in the western suburb of Beijing. Majestic in scale, its architecture magnificent, the monastery is the largest in the suburbs of Beijing and was built to follow the contours of the mountain. The Buddhist buildings lead on from each other up the hill in picturesque disorder, the large Precious Hall of the Great Hero at the highest point. Five bays wide and with a double-eaved palatial-like roof, its central bays have hung on the upper and lower eaves horizontal boards inscribed with golden characters; "Peace, quiet and dignified," is to be read on the upper board; "Happiness like the sea and pearls like the wheel of the Law," on the lower one. A vast platform with stone balustrades and a flight of marble steps extends in front of the hall. Dating from the Qing Dynasty, a huge and stately statue of Sakyamuni Buddha, flanked by statues of Ananda and Kasayapa, is enshrined in the centre of the hall, and overhead are wonderfully sculptured exotic birds, dragons, lions, elephants and sheep.

Dougong Bracket Patterns in the Precious Hall of the Great Hero in the Tanzhe Temple, Beijing

The Precious Hall of the Great Hero is the principal building in the Tanzhe Temple. Richly decorated, its roof is covered with glazed yellow tiles and has a border of green. At both ends of the central ridge, huge glazed zoomorphic ornaments in the form of monstrous animals are to be seen, each bound by long and glittering chains of fine gold. It is said that when Emperor Kangxi first came to the Tanzhe Temple, fearing that the animals were about to fly off into the sky, he ordered them to be fettered with gold chains. These resplendent ornaments, reputed to be relics of the Yuan Dynasty, are full of life and realistically worked; true masterpieces of the art. The upper and lower eaves of the Precious hall of the Great Hero have exquisitely decorated dougong brackets in green and gold. Three layers of colourful brackets are piled up on top of each other and golden dragons embellish the beams and square pillars.

Pagoda Forest in the Tanzhe Temple, Beijing

The Tanzhe Temple is the temple in Beijing with the longest history. It is also the largest in the Beijing suburbs. It was first built during the Western Jin Dynasty (265-317) and was initially called the "Jiafu Monastery." By the time of the Tang Dynasty, it had been extended, used for Buddhist lectures and renamed "Longquan si" (dragon spring temple). In the 11th year of the reign of Kangxi, Emperor Shengzu of the Qing Dynasty, it was called the Xiuyun Chan Monastery upon imperial order, but was still popularly known as the Tanzhe Temple. Its principal buildings were built along the left, middle and right three roads. In addition to the main building complex, there is also "Anle Hall" in front of the temple gate for monks to live out their retirement. In front of the monastery, there are the upper and lower pagoda yards, as well as monks' tomb pagodas dating from the Liao, Jin, Ming and Qing dynasties. They are the tombs of well-known abbots and eminent Chan masters of past generations. Shown here is the stone pagoda forest in a pagoda yard.

Pagoda Forest in the Tanzhe Temple, Beijing

Located in the quiet setting of a mountain forest, the Tanzhe Temple is a restful and appealing place, with the monastic buildings perfectly integrated into the natural environment. In addition to the principal buildings such as the Precious Hall of the Great Hero, Pilu Tower and Guangyin Yard, its pagoda forest and yard are also famous. In the latter, scores of tomb pagodas for the Buddhist monks of the Liao, Jin, Ming and Qing dynasties are to be seen. The different-sized pagodas in the pagoda forest, the largest in Beijing, are mostly close-eaved and built of brick and stone. To be seen here is a view of the pagoda forest in the Tanzhe Temple.

120

Diamond Throne Pagoda in the Biyun Monastery, Beijing

The Biyun (azure cloud) Monastery is situated at the eastern foot of the Western Hills in Beijing. Composed of six yards, the whole monastery was built on the mountain slope. The principal building, Sakyamuni Hall, built in the Ming Dynasty has an exquisitely decorated caisson ceiling. Shown here is the Diamond Throne Pagoda. Built in the 13th year of the reign of Qianlong (1748), Emperor Gaozong of the Qing Dynasty, the pagoda is located at the highest point. Built along the lines of the Wuta (five pagoda) Monastery outside Xizhimen in Beijing, it is 34.7 m high and over the base is a three-storeyed stand. The pagoda base is square, of brick and stone, and surfaced with a kind of black-spotted stone. On both sides of the base are sculptured balustrades. In 1925, Dr. SunYat-sen passed away in Beijing. His dead body was entombed temporarily in the base of the Diamond Throne Pagoda . Later, his coffin was moved to Nanjing and only his hat and suit of clothes were left here. Inside the monastery is the Dr. Sun Yat-sen memorial hall.

Detail of the Diamond Throne Pagoda in the Biyun Monastery, Beijing

The whole Diamond Throne Pagoda in the Biyun Monastery was built of carved and polished marble stone. Sculpted Buddhist statues, typical of Tibetan Lamaism, surround the pagoda. An arched entrance, flanked by statues of Buddha, its sides decorated with animal head patterns, is located in the centre of the pagoda base. Stone steps lead from inside the archway to the top of the throne, which has seven stone pagodas standing on it. In the foreground, to the left and right, are round stupas, and behind these stand five thirteen-storeyed square pagodas with close eaves, arranged dice-like, with the central one being the largest. A kind of scripture altar, it represents a unique style of architecture. The stand of each pagoda is a Sumeru throne and above it, the so-called belly is decorated with richly carved statues of Buddha. The thirteen Wheels of the Law are topped by a bronze canopy. A smaller pagoda sits on top of this, hollowed out to provide room for a Buddha.

Diamond Throne Pagoda in the Greater Zhengjue Monastery, Beijing
opposite page

The Greater Zhengjue Monastery is situated outside Xizhimen in Beijing and is famous for its Diamond Throne Pagoda. Also known as the Wuta Monastery, the Diamond Throne Pagoda is a type of Buddhist Pagoda to be found in China. The Buddha Ghaya pagoda in India, built to commemorate Sakyamuni attaining Buddhahood, served as model. Built of brick and marble, the pagoda here is divided into the lower precious throne (the base) and the upper five pagodas. Of the five extant diamond throne pagodas in China, three are in Beijing: the diamond throne pagoda in the Biyun Monastery, the Qingjing Huacheng in the Western Huangsi Monastery and the pagoda shown here, which is the earliest, the sculptures on the outside walls the most finely executed.

Detail of the Diamond Throne Pagoda in the Greater Zhengjue Monastery, Beijing

The Greater Zhengjue Monastery was first built during the reign of Yongle (1403-1424), Emperor Chenfzu of the Ming Dynasty. The Diamond Throne Pagoda was built later and on the lintel of the archway we are told that the pagoda was built in the 9th year of the reign of Chenghua (1473), Emperor Xianzong of the Ming Dynasty. The whole pagoda is divided into two parts: the precious throne (the base) and the stone pagoda. The former is built of brick with marble stone facing on the outside. Rising to a height of 7.7 m, the pagoda throne is divided into six storeys, separated by projecting eaves. Tapering slowly upwards, each storey has a row of Buddhist niches. Four small pagodas stand on top with a large thirteen-storeyed one in the centre. They are 7 m high and divided into 11 storeys. These five pagodas are obeliscal in shape symbolizing Mount Sumeru, the residence of Buddha. In style, they resemble the close-eaved pagoda of the Tang Dynasty.

The Glazed Archway in the Wofo Monastery, Beijing

Situated at the northern foot of the Western Hills, 10 km northwest of Beijing, the Wofo (sleeping Buddha) Monastery was built in the first year of the reign of Zhenguan (627-649), Emperor Taizong of the Tang Dynasty. Originally called Doushuai Monastery, it was later expanded and in the 12th year of the reign of Yongzheng (1734), Emperor Shizong of the Qing Dynasty, renamed Shifang Pujue. Due to the giant Sleeping Buddha within its walls, it became known throughout the world as the Sleeping Buddha Monastery. The monastery is laid out within an extensive courtyard and the glazed archway to be seen in the picture is located in front, set off by the verdant hills surrounding it. Inside the temple gate, there are four courtyards containing four Buddhist buildings. They are in order of precedence, the Hall of the Heavenly King, Hall of the Three-generation Buddha, Hall of the Sleeping Buddha and the Scripture Tower, of which the most famous is the Hall of the Sleeping Buddha. The picture shows the glazed archway outside the Sleeping Buddha Monastery. Three bays wide and four bays deep, with seven towers, it is a superb example of the art of fine carving, be it on stone, tiles or wood.

The Glazed Archway of the Lama Temple, Beijing

Located in the northeast corner of Andingmen in Beijing, the Lama temple is the largest in scale and the best preserved. Originally it was the mansion of the would-be Emperor Yongzheng of the Qing Dynasty. In the third year of the reign of Yongzheng of the Qing Dynasty, it was given the name of Yonghegong Palace. On Yongzheng's death, his coffin was placed in the palace, its green tiled roof, typical for mansions, converted and given the imperial yellow glazed tiles. In the ninth year of the reign of Qianlong (1744), Emperor Gaozong of the Qing Dynasty, the place was formally declared a Lama temple. The buildings are arranged along a long axis running from south to north with southern exposure. The overall layout is strict and precise with a clear central axis. The picture shows one of the first three glazed archways of the Lama temple. Three bays wide and four columns with seven tops, its dougong brackets are particularly splendid with their elegant carving and colourful patterning.

Wanfu Tower in the Lama Temple, Beijing

Five grand halls represent the principal buildings of the extensive Lama temple. Wanfu (ten-thousand blessings) Tower is located in the last courtyard and is the tallest building. Seen externally, it is a two-storeyed tower with three eaves. Standing at about 30 m, it is a tall-looking building, also known as the Tower of the Giant Buddha on account of the statue of Maitreya being enshrined here. It is flanked by the Yongkang and Yansui towers, all three connected on the second storey by two, three-bay passageways, which rise slightly as they join up with the Wanfu tower. The idea behind the architecturally interesting technique of joining up three towers to make one was to express paradise, a palace as the home of the immortal, also known as the Tower of the Heavenly Palace.

Statue of Maitreya Buddha in Wanfu Tower in the Lama Temple, Beijing
opposite page

Wanfu Tower is a three-storeyed hollow Buddhist hall containing the enshrined 24 m high statue of Maitreya Buddha. It is a majestic sculpture, carved out of a single piece of white sandalwood given as a gift to the Emperor Qianlong by Dalai Lama VII. The detailed carving of the robe and jewellery, the inlaid pearls and jade, the soft draperies over the arms, fluttering gently when a draught arises, make the statue an absolute masterpiece. The internal structure of the Wanfu tower manifests a sophisticated building technique used during the Qing Dynasty and based on the lessons of the past. Glorious, too, is the highly ornate caisson ceiling.

Guanyin Tower in the Dule Monastery, Jixian, Tianjin

The Dule Monastery is located in Jixian County of Tianjin, 90 km east of Beijing. It was reputedly first built during the first years of the Tang Dynasty. In the 14th year of the reign of Tianbao (741), Xuanzong of the Tang Dynasty, a certain An Lushan plotted a rebellion and a mass pledge was taken here. The place was therefore called the Dule Monastery, and comprises three parts; the east, west and middle. Houses for the Buddhist monks, and a former temporary residence for the emperor are to be found in the east and west sections, whereas the middle one represents the monastery's main section, with an axis running from south to north by the temple gate and Guanyin Tower. This layout was typical of the Tang Dynasty, whereby the Buddhist buildings formed the centre of the monastery, with winding corridors connecting them with the temple gate. The corridors here unfortunately no longer exist. The Guanyin Tower we see today is the one rebuilt in the 2nd year of the reign of Tonghe (984) of the Liao Dynasty. Seen historically, it comes only second to the Eastern Great Hall of the Foguang Monastery in Wutai, Shanxi Province, but it is the earliest wooden tower in China. Of solid and noble appearance, it has stood the test of time, even surviving 28 earthquakes - a proud testimony indeed to the excellence of ancient Chinese architecture.

Lateral View of Guanyin Tower in the Dule Monastery, Jixian, Tianjin

22.5 m high and 20.23 m wide, Guanyin Tower seen externally is five bays wide with eight structural frames. It is a two-storeyed tower with a single-eaved roof and a balcony running round the upper storey. A series of dougong brackets can be seen on the first and second storeys as well as under the roof. The plan and elevation of the tower are strictly in proportion, lending the building elegant harmony. Structurally, it is similar to the wooden pagoda of Yingxian in Shanxi Province. Here, three rectangular circular structures are piled up so that an open space running through the three storeys is created in the middle to house the 16 m high Guanyin statue in the tower. Here is a form of tower structure that is typical of the Liao Dynasty.

Statue of Guanyin in the Dule Monastery, Jixian, Tianjin / opposite page

On the Sumeru throne in the middle of Guanyin Tower an eleven-faced clay Guanyin statue of the Liao Dynasty stands aloft. At 16 m, it is the tallest extant clay-sculptured statue in China, completely filling the inner space of the tower. Of solemn bearing, the body of the Buddhist statue leans slightly forward, with Bodhisattvas on either side offering sacrifices. The statue is a perfect reflection of the artistic style prevalent in the then flourishing Tang Dynasty. To accommodate the Guanyin statue, an open space was created extending over three storeys. At first square, it becomes hexagonal at third storey level, to end in an octagonal caisson ceiling. Daylight streams through an opening on the third storey to light up the statue's face. The atmosphere is deeply spiritual.

Central Cave Ceiling of the Resonant Mountain, Handan, Hebei

In the Gushan Mountain southwest of Handan City, there are sixteen stone caves containing more than 3,000 statues. The caves are deep, and the stone is firm and fine in quality. The name 'Resonant Hall' is used in connection with the caves on account of the excellent acoustics. Located both at the southern foot and the central part of Gushan, the caves are divided into the southern and northern ones. The northern one has nine storeys and this nine-storeyed, octagonal brick pagoda marks the main part of the complex. The Northern Resonant Mountain has nine caves, of which three were built in the Northern Qi Dynasty (550-577), the rest being relics of the Sui, Tang, Song and Ming dynasties. Of the nine caves, the largest is the sixth (Big Buddha cave) and the statues are more or less completely preserved. The excellence of the carving has resulted in sculptures of grotesque animals and flying apsaras as well as of the Heavenly King and bodhisattva that are extremely lifelike. In the picture is the ceiling of the northern Resonant Cave.

The White Pagoda in the Guanyin Monastery, Jixian, Tianjin

The Guanyin Monastery is located in Jixian County, Tianjin. The White Pagoda stands on the axis hundreds of metres south of the Dule Monastery. It is not clear when the monastery was built, but the White Pagoda dates from the Liao Dynasty. According to "A Survey of Jizhou," the monastery was reconstructed in the 60th year of the reign of Qianlong, Emperor Gaozong of the Qing Dynasty, and the original style was preserved when reconstruction took place. The White Pagoda is octagonal in plan, with each side of the pagoda base 4.58 m long. Rising to a height of 30.6 m, the structure is unusual. Set on top of the pagoda base is the octagonal first storey with eight small pagodas set in relievo at each corner. Doors are positioned on the north, south, east and west sides, the one facing south able to be opened, revealing a small room in the centre of the pagoda. The other four sides have tablets, again in relievo, engraved with Buddhist hymns. The second and third storeys are of different height. The first, second and third storeys are close-eave in form. The pagoda ends in a plump stupa spire.

Bell Tower of the Xiantong Monastery on Mt. Wutai, Wutai, Shanxi

The Xiantong Monastery is located on Mt. Wutai in Shanxi Province. As it was said to resemble the Divine Vulture Peak in India, the monastery was originally given the name of Greater Lingjiu (greater divine vulture). The bell tower of the Xiantong Monastery is at the southeast corner, outside the monastery. Two storeys high, its lower part consists of an archway for pedestrians to go through. The lower storey has projecting eaves and the upper one comprises a big bell tower of wooden structure with double eaves and cross ridge. On the west side of the second storey is a passageway connecting the tower with the granary courtyard in front of the temple gate. A huge bronze bell hangs in the bell tower. Cast during the reign of Tianqi (1621-1627), Emperor Xizong of the Ming Dynasty, it is said to weigh 9,999.5 kg is 2.5 m tall, 9.9 cm thick and 1.65 m in outer diameter. More than 10,000 words are engraved on the outside of the bell recounting Buddhist scriptures. The sonorous toll of the big bell can be heard in the township of Taihuai, far away in Wutai County.

Pagoda in the Tayuan Monastery on Mt. Wutai, Wutai, Shanxi

The Tayuan Monastery is situated south of the Xiantong Monastery. It is one of the five important places for Buddhist meditation on the mountain. During the Tang Dynasty, it was part of the Greater Huayan Monastery together with the Xiantong Monastery. In the 5th year of the reign of Yongle (1407), Emperor Chengzu of the Ming Dynasty, they were divided into two. The White Pagoda of the Tayuan Monastery is also known as the Cishou Pagoda. A relic from the cremation of Sakyamuni is kept inside. The base of the pagoda is square with a perimeter more than 80 m in length. The lower part has a long corridor running round it and four small pavilions stand at the four corners. The pagoda is more than 50 m high and is topped by a robust-looking Buddhist Wheel of the Law. The wheel is placed over a round bronze plate 23 m in perimeter with 35 rectangular-shaped bronze plates hanging down from its edge and a bronze treasure bottle, 5.4 m high, rising upwards from its centre. 252 bells that jingle in the breeze hang from the pagoda's sides, producing a pleasant sound. The pagoda has became a symbol of the Holy Land of Buddhism on Mt. Wutai.

The Precious Hall of the Great Hero in the Xiantong Monastery on Mt. Wutai, Wutai, Shanxi / opposite page

First built during the reign of Yongping (58-75), Emperor Mingdi of the Eastern Han Dynasty, the monastery was the earliest to be built on Mt. Wutai. When it was renovated during the reign of Emperor Taizu of the Ming Dynasty, it was granted the right to display a horizontal board bearing the words, "Greater Xiantong Monastery" and became one of the five important locations for Buddhist meditation on Mt. Wutai. The monastery covers an area of more than 100 mu (6.46 hm^2) and along the central axis stand seven Buddhist buildings, of more than 400 bays. Grand in scale, most were renovated and reconstructed during the Ming and Qing dynasties. The Precious Hall of the Great Hero is in the third courtyard. Rebuilt in the 25th year of the reign of Guangxu (1899), Emperor Dezeng of the Qing Dynasty, it is a place for important Buddhist ceremonies in the monastery.

Veranda of the Precious Hall of the Great Hero in Pusading on Mt. Wutai, Wutai, Shanxi / left

Traditional Chinese architecture is governed by laws that, for instance, regulate the height of the platforms, the number of bays and style of roof. Buddhist monasteries are no exception. Thus according to the regulations of the Ming and Qing dynasties, only the imperial palaces, mausoleums and buildings erected upon imperial order were allowed to use yellow glazed tiles in order to display their honorable standing. Monasteries on Mt. Wutai therefore all use grey brick and grey tile. Pusading forms an exception as it was used as occasional residence by the Qing Dynasty emperors. The temple gate and the Buddhist buildings, therefore, all have roofs of yellow glazed tiles. The area between the beams and square pillars is covered with colourful paintings depicting dragons and other scenes. Compared with the architecture of the Ming Dynasty, Pusading, also called the 'miniature Potala Palace' on account of its attractiveness, has an imposing beauty. To be seen in the picture is the veranda in front of the Precious Hall of the Great Hero.

The Precious Hall of the Great Hero in Pusading on Mt. Wutai, Wutai, Shanxi / right

Situated on top of Lingjiu peak, northwest of Taihuai Township on Mt. Wutai, Pusading was first built during the reign of Emperor Xiaowen (471) of the Northen Wei Dynasty. It initially bore the name of Greater Wenshu (Manjusri). In the fifth year of the reign of Zhenguan (631), Emperor Taizong of the Tang Dynasty, it was renamed the Zhenrong Monastery. In the first year of the reign of Yongle, Emperor Chengzu of the Ming Dynasty, it reverted to its former name. Renovated in the ninth year of the reign of Wanli (1581), Emperor Shenzong of the Ming Dynasty, it reached its prime in the Qing Dynasty. The monastery covers an area of 9,100 m^2 with more than 120 bays. As one of the five Buddhist meditation sites in Wutai, it is the largest Lamaist monastery on Mt.Wutai, and one of the yellow monasteries on Mt. Wutai. Stone steles stand in abundance within the monastery walls, and ancient cypresses soar upwards. The Buddhist buildings are not large in scale but have a primitive strength, unadorned as they are, and majesty. It is said that the monastery's chief lama was made a provincial commander by Emperor Kangxi, and the standing this implied is reflected in the layout of the monastery.

Hall of the Great Buddha in the Nanchan Monastery of Mt. Wutai, Wutai, Shanxi

It is not clear when the Nanchan Monastery was built. The Great Buddha hall, however, was renovated and reconstructed in the third year of the reign of Jianzhong (782), Emperor Dezong of the Tang Dynasty. In the 5th year of the reign of Huichang (845), when Emperor Wuzong of the Tang Dynasty ordered that Buddhism be annihilated, more than 40,000 Buddhist monasteries were destroyed throughout China, and although Mt. Wutai was equally affected, the Nanchan Monastery survived by sheer luck, because it was not known. Its Great Buddha Hall is the oldest surviving wooden building in China. It faces south, is three bays wide and three bays deep. Seventeen statues of bodhisattva dating from the Tang Dynasty are enshrined in the columnless hall. The roof slopes gently and has wide eaves on all four sides. The corners of the roof are supported by a group of beautifully carved dougong brackets left in their natural state.

General Plan and Section of the Nanchan Monastery and Restored Elevation and Section of the Great Hall

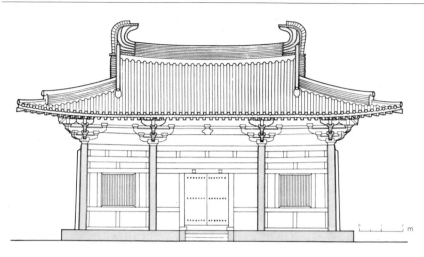

Restored Elevation of the Great Hall in the Nan-Chan Monastery

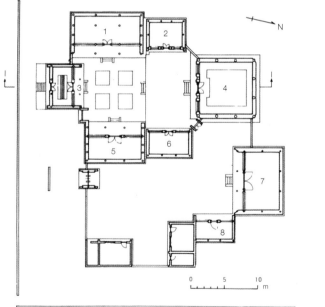

1. Arhat Hall
2. Dhama Protection Hall
3. Temple Gate
4. Great Hall
5. Ghalan Hall
6. Guanyin Hall
7. Palace of King of hell
8. Eastern Chan House

General Plan of the Nan-Chan Monastery

Located west of the villages of Lijiazhuang, 22 km southwest of Wutai County City in Shanxi Province, the Nanchan Monastery faces south. In addition to the Great Hall, the monastery also consists of the temple gate, the Arhat Hall, the Ghalan Hall, the Dharma Protection Hall, the Guanyin Hall, the Hall of the King of Hell, the Eastern Chan House and other principal buildings, forming a quadrangle or enclosed on four sides. The Great Hall was built in the 3rd year of the reign of Jianzhong (782) of the Tang dynasty. It is the earliest wooden-structured building still in existence in China. Three-bays wide and three-bays deep, its plan is approximately square. With single-eave and grey-tiled sloped roofing (roof slope is 1:5. 15), it represents the smoothest known of the roofs with a wooden structure built in ancient times. The central bay of the front eave has been given a plank door whereas the bays on either side have a latticed window and the other sides remain closed. The beam structure is simple with the column top having only one inner lintel. The roof has a gentle slope and wide overhanging eaves. It is a beautiful and well-proportioned building and an excellent example of the typical wooden-structured style of the Tang dynasty.

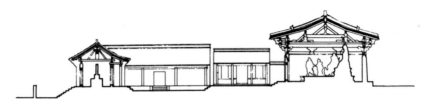

Section of the Nan-Chan Monastery

0 1 2 3 4 m

Restored Section of the Great Hall in the Nanchan Monastery

Eastern Great Hall of the Foguang Monastery on Mt. Wutai, Wutai, Shanxi

The Foguang (Buddhist light) Monastery was first built during the reign of Emperor Xiaowen (471-499) of the Northern Wei Dynasty and flourished for a time during the Tang Dynasty. It is one of the important monasteries on Mt. Wutai. A three-storeyed Maitreya hall, seven bays wide and 32 m high, originally stood on the site, but was destroyed during the persecution of Buddhism that took place during the reign of Huichang. In the 11th year of the reign of Dazhong (857), Emperor Xuangzong of the Tang Dynasty, it was rebuilt by a woman from Chang'an, becoming the Eastern Great Hall of today. Following the physical features of the land, the layout of the Foguang Monastery is arranged along the axis running from east to west. The temple gate is located on the west side, which is flat and low. Also known as Weituo Hall, the magnificent Eastern Great Hall is located on the eastern platform, the highest place. The terrace in front of the hall lies 20 m above the preceding courtyard.

Close Shot of the Eastern Great Hall in the Foguang Monastery on Mt. Wutai, Wutai, Shanxi

The Eastern Great Hall is seven bays wide and 34 m long. The five central bays of the front eave have been given plank doors. The last two bays at each end have a low wall, on top of which are straight lattice windows. The great hall is four bays deep and 17.66 m wide with thick and solid gables. In front of the hall stairs stand two large and ancient pines. On the axis between the trees stands a scripture pillar, erected in the 11th year of the reign of Dazhong (857), Emperor Xuanzong of the Tang Dynasty and inscribed with the name of the woman who built the Eastern Great Hall. The hall itself is single-eaved with a palatial top. The dougong brackets below the eaves are simple and unadorned, the ones on top of the capitals four-layered and jutting out. Between the two columns, is another group of brackets over the subsidiary bay. The eave columns incline slightly inwards , the corner columns slightly higher. The elevation and front of the Great Hall are thus given a striking rhythm and beautiful curve.

General Plan and Section of the Foguang Monastery, Front Elevation and Section of the Great Hall

1. Manjusri Hall
2. Hall of Heavenly King
3. Scripture Pillar of the reign of Qianfu of Tang
4. Scripture Pillar of the reign of Dazhong of Tang
5. Great Hall
6. Ghalan Hall
7. Founder Pagoda

General Plan of the Foguang Monastery

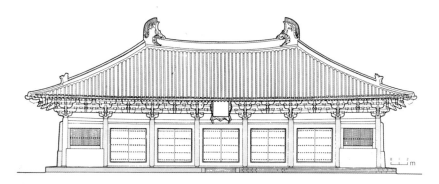

Front Elevation of the Great Hall in the Foguang Monastery

The Foguang Monastery is located 30 km northeast of Wutai County in Shanxi Province. Nestling halfway up a mountain, it faces west with its central axis from east to west. In a beautiful and peaceful setting, surrounded as it is by pines and cypresses , the monastery boasts a great variety of architecture in the form of over 120 temple buildings, towers and pavilions. Due to the lie of land, the overall plan of the whole monastery consists of three terraces, each higher than the other. The first terrace is rather wide. On the central axis stands a stone pillar inscribed with Tuoluoni scripture dating from the 4th year of the reign of Qianfu (877), Emperor Xizong of the Tang Dynasty. To the north is Manjusri Hall built in the 15th year of the reign of Tianhui (1137) of the Jin Dynasty. To the south and in symmetry with it was Guanyin Hall (another version was Samanthabhadra Hall), no longer in existence. On both sides of the central axis are corridors running round the second terrace and a side courtyard, all built in modern times. The third terrace was given a retaining wall, and in the very middle stands the Eastern Great Hall built in the Tang Dynasty. Directly in front of it, in a central position, stands the scripture pillar erected in the 11th year of the reign of Dazhong of the Tang Dynasty. To its southeast is the founder pagoda and on both sides are the side halls built in the past few years. The Great Hall of the Foguang Monastery represents the most important building of the monastery. Although of great simplicity, the Great Hall is a magnificent building, seven-bays (34 m) wide and four - bays (11.66 m) deep. It has a single-eaved roof, its contour smooth, and made all the more attractive by the large and dramatic dougong brackets. The pillar height and width of bay are almost identical. The front facade has its central bay and the two bays on either side provided with plank doors and the remaining bay at each end with a latticed window. The walls are otherwise unbroken. The foundation to the rear was formed by excavating the cliff behind, and because the foundation in front is lower, the pillar shafts are longer at the front of the building than at the back. Dougong brackets have been applied directly to the pillar caps. The central ridge extends the width of three bays and its two ends are located above the joints of the beam structure so that the latter shoulders the weight of the beam ends. The overall composition of the central ridge, roof, beam ends and the structure as a whole is harmonious and immensely satisfying.

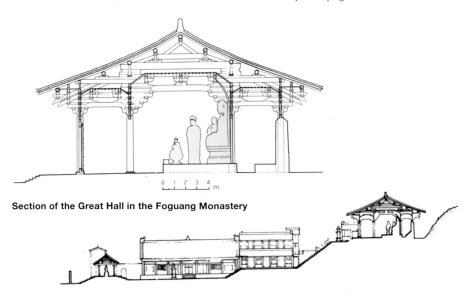

0 1 2 3 4 m

Section of the Great Hall in the Foguang Monastery

Section of the Foguang Monastery

Schematic Drawing of the Beam Structure of the Great Hall in the Foguang Monastery

Of all the Buddhist buildings built during the Tang Dynasty, the Great Hall of the Foguang Monastery is the oldest, most typical and most magnificent still in existence. It is seven-bays wide and four-bays deep. Structurally the Great Hall comprises three components; the lower part (pillar net), the middle part (fixture part) and the upper part (top structure).

The pillar net is the basic structural layer composed of inner and outer peripheral pillars forming an inner trough five-bays wide and two-bays deep and a peripheral outer trough. All the many structural members of the Great hall are closely integrated, each playing its own important role.

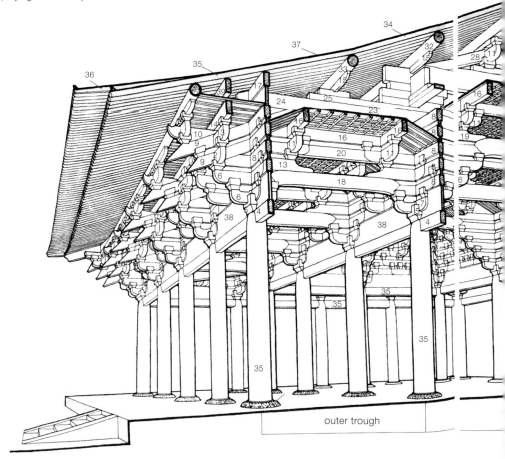

outer trough

General Plan of the Great Hall in the Foguang Monastery

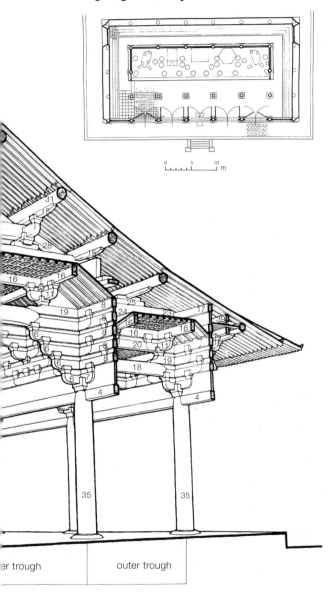

0   5   10
|...|...| m

1. column base
2. eave column
3. inner trough column
4. inner lintel
5. bolu bracket
6. transverse bracket arm
7. lowest longitudinal bracket arm
8. column cap square
9. lower cantilever arm
10. bird's beak-end
11. longitudinal bracket arm carrying the eave purlin
12. lowest longitudinal bracket arm
13. transverse bracket arm
14. arhat tie
15. substitution board
16. flat cheese square
17. rafter overhanging the trough
18. extension beam
19. beam pad in semi-humpshape
20. plain square pillar
21. four-rafter beam
22. beam pad in hump shape
23. plan coffer ceiling
24. hidden beam
25. auxiliary beam
26. four-rafter hidden beam
27. flat beam
28. side brace
29. slanting beam
30. ridge rafter
31. upper flat rafter
32. mid-flat rafter
33. lower flat rafter
34. rafter
35. eave rafter
36. flying rafter
37. roof boarding
38. wall between dougong
39. cowback rafter

er trough   outer trough

Detail of the Flying Rainbow Pagoda in the Upper Guangsheng Monastery, Hongdong, Shanxi

The Flying Rainbow Pagoda began to be built in the 10th year of the reign of Zhengde (1515), Emperor Wuzong of the Ming Dynasty. Taking 12 years to build, it was completed in the 6th year of the reign of Jiajing (1527) of the Ming Dynasty. An octagonal pagoda, it has 13 storeys. The body of the pagoda is constructed of brick, its facade given a seven-colour glaze. Glazed dougong brackets, the column caps, an abundance of meti-culously sculpted figures, Buddhas, bodhisattva, warriors, attendants, writhing dragons, birds, floral patterns and the musical instruments used in the Buddhist mass that decorate the first three storeys perfectly illustrate Ming Dynasty skill in glaze manufacturing.

Flying Rainbow Pagoda of the Upper Guangsheng Monastery, Hongdong, Shanxi
opposite page

First built in the Eastern Han Dynasty, the Guangsheng Monastery is divided into an upper and lower part, located respectively on top and at the foot of Mt. Huoshan. It came to be called by its present name in the 4th year of the reign of Dali (769), Emperor Taizong of the Tang Dynasty when it was renovated and reconstructed. Later, due to additions made during the dynasties that followed, it became a sizeable monastery complex. The upper monastery includes many courtyards and on its axis lie the temple gate, the Flying Rainbow Pagoda, Maituo Hall, the Precious Hall of the Great Hero, Pilu Hall and other edifices. The Buddhist buildings still in existence in the upper monastery are mostly Ming, but the Buddhist statues date primarily from the Yuan Dynasty. The Flying Rainbow Pagoda stands between the temple gate and Maituo Hall. It is a typical Ming monastic brick pagoda in the form of a tower, octagonal in plan with a wooden corridor running round the bottom storey.

Drawings of the Great Hall in the Lower Guangsheng Monastery and its Framework Structure

Lower Guangsheng Monastery is located at the foot of Mt. Huoshan, 17 km northeast of Hongdong County, Shanxi Province. It consists of the temple gate, front hall, back hall (Great Hall) and the side halls.

The principal hall, the Great Hall, was rebuilt in the 2nd year of the reign of Zhida (1309) of the Yuan Dynasty. It is seven bays wide and four bays deep, and has a hanging roof with one tier of eaves. The three central bays have been given doors whereas the two bays on either side have lattice windows and the rear section and the gables. All the hypostyle columns in the front trough of the subsidiary and intermediate bays are dispensed with, while in the rear trough, the two bays were made to share one hypostyle column standing at the centre of the intermediate bay. Thus, with only six hypostyle columns in the hall, much space was gained.

The beam framework of the Great Hall of the Lower Guangsheng Monastery has two main characteristics. First, it used fewer columns in the hall and made some changes regarding their positioning. The number of bays divided by the columns is less than that of the beam framework. The beam framework, therefore, was not set directly on the columns, but a large horizontal inner lintel was placed on the inner column to support the beam framework. To increase the space for activities in the front part of the hall, two columns were dispensed with at both sides. Due to this, and to support the beam framework above, the two large lintels were lengthened to 11.5 m. Secondly, slanting beams were used. The lower part of the slanting beam was placed on the corbel brackets and the upper end on the inner lintel, covered with rafters, thus saving a beam. This bold and flexible structural method was characteristic of the architecture of the Yuan Dynasty.

A feature, too, of the architecture of the late Yuan or early Ming dynasties was the large cantilever arm, sometimes employed instead of a beam. Such a feature is to be seen in the Great Hall of the Lower Guangsheng Monastery.

Elevation of the Great Hall in the Lower Guangsheng Monastery

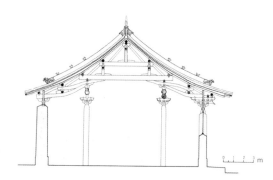

Horizontal Section of the Lower Guangsheng Monastery

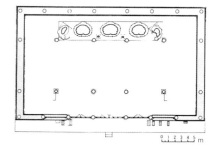

Plan of the Great Hall in the Lower Guangsheng Monastery

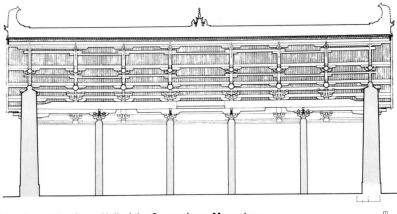

Vertical Section of the Great Hall of the Guangsheng Monastery

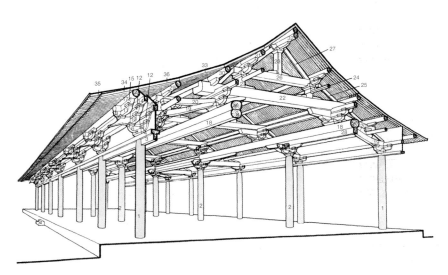

Drawing of the Beams and Framework of the Great Hall of the Guangsheng Monastery

1. eave column
2. inner column
3. horizontal inner lintel
4. rectangular plate lintel
5. bolu bracket
6. transverse bracket arm
7. cantilever arm
8. bird's beak-end
9. the first longitudinal bracket arm

10. the lowest longitudinal bracket arm
11. longitudinal bracket arm carrying the eave purlin
12. the first transverse bracket arm
13. column head rafter
14. arhat tie
15. subsititutiona board
16. board covering the rafter

17. rafter projecting eave
18. inner lintel
19. slanting beam
20. connecting beam
21. hump-shaped beam pad
22. four-rafter beam
23. Shuzhu post
24. a regular square device
25. side brace
26. flat beam

27. slanting beam
28. Zhuomu rafter
29. lower flat rafter
30. mid-flat rafter
31. upper flat rafter
32. ridge rafter
33. rafter
34. eave rafter
35. flying rafter
36. roof boarding

151

Detail of the Outer Eaves of the Sakya Pagoda in the Fogong Monastery, Yingxian, Shanxi

The body of the Sakya Pagoda is actually large, but due to the external corridors and flying eaves on each storey, it does not appear cumbersome and the shadows cast by the dougong brackets, eaves and projecting external corridors even create a rhythmic effect. Seen from the outside, the pagoda has five storeys, but structurally it has nine. Of these, four are concealed between the upper flat base of the external corridors and the dougong brackets below, forming a hollow double-storeyed circular structure. Between the inner columns of the concealed storey and the inner and outer corner columns diagonal stays act as a support. Like a reinforced ring, this effectively strengthens the whole structure of the pagoda. The hollow part in the middle provides space to accommodate the giant Buddhist statue.

Sakya Pagoda in the Fogong Monastery, Yingxian, Shanxi / opposite page

The Sakya Pagoda stands in the middle of the central axis of the Fogong Monastery. In front is the temple gate and behind the Great Hall, in keeping with the traditional style of Buddist monastery layout of the Northern and Southern Dynasties. Built in the 2nd year of the reign of Qing Ning (1056) of the Liao Dynasty, it is the oldest wooden Buddhist pagoda still in existence in China. Reaching a height of 67.3 m, it has, when seen from the outside, five storeys. The lowest is double-eaved and surrounded by a corridor. From the second storey upwards, the diametre is gradually reduced making the pagoda taper elegantly upwards. The whole is crowned by a 14 m high spire. The fine black dots in the picture are little birds flying around the pagoda.

Outer Eave Corridor of the Sakya Pagoda in the Fogong Monastery, Yingxian, Shanxi

Buddhist statues are enshrined on each storey. The gold statue of Sakyamuni on the first is 11 m high, those on the other floors much smaller. Sixty different types of dougong bracket are used throughout the pagoda. Two circles of vertical columns rise up inside the edifice, the inner circle with eight columns, the outer with twenty-four, resulting in a double-layered tubular structure. The space enclosed by the inner columns is the Buddhist hall, that between the inner and outer columns forming a corridor for worshippers to perambulate. Outside is an external corridor or balcony running round each floor. The pagoda has stood for 950 years, and the fact that it has survived several earthquakes is proof of the structural quality of ancient Chinese architecture.

Cupboard in the Bojia Scripture Hall of the Lower Huayan Monastery, Datong, Shanxi

The Bojia Scripture Hall in the Lower Huayan Monastery was built in the 7th year of the reign of Chongxi (1038), Emperor Xingzong of the Liao Dynasty. The great hall faces east, is five bays wide and four bays deep with single-eaved sloped roofing. Right in the middle of the great hall a Buddhist statue is enshrined. Along the two gables and its rear wall 38 scripture cupboards in the form of a storeyed-tower have been provided, each superimposed by a Buddhist niche. The lower part serves as a cupboard for scriptures. The construction above is a perfect miniature replica of traditional architecture with the external corridors, overhanging eaves, dougong brackets, roof, roof beams and zoomorphic ornaments all to be seen. Outstanding is the Heavenly Palace scripture cupboard placed above a window in the centre of the rear wall. Taking the form of a five-bay tower with arched bridges connecting it to the cupboards on the left and right, it is a rare example of Liao Dynasty wooden architecture. (Photo by Sun Dazhang)

Interior View of the Precious Hall of the Great Hero in the Upper Huayan Monastery, Datong, Shanxi

Built during the Liao and Jin dynasties, the Huayan Monastery includes an upper and a lower monastery. The two complexes are close to each other. The Precious Hall of the Great Hero is the principal Buddhist building of the upper monastery. Built in the 3rd year of the reign of Tianjuan (1140), Emperor Xizong of the Jin Dynasty, it is a palatial, single-eaved building. The gently sloping roof has great overhanging eaves and large zoomorphic ornaments decorate each end of its central ridge. The great hall is 9 bays wide and five bays deep. Extending over an area of 1,560 m², it is the largest single-eaved timbered building of ancient China. The inner columns, taller than those supporting the eaves, are few, so as to allow more space in the interior for arranging the Buddhist statues and allowing believers to pay their respects. The five main statues in the great hall date from the Ming Dynasty.

Interior View of Cave No. 51 of the Yungang Grottoes, Datong, Shanxi

Located at the foot of Wuzhou Mountain west of Datong City, the Yungang Grottoes have been hollowed out of a stretch of mountain extending for almost one km in an east-westerly direction. Grand in scale, only 53 caves now remain containing more than 51,000 statues of Buddha, Bodhisattva, flying fairies and other statues. The picture shows the entrance to Cave No. 51. Like Cave No.1, 2, 6, and others, it belongs to the category of the square cave. Inside are independent stone pagoda pillars in the form of a storeyed tower. Among them the best preserved is in Cave No. 2. The pagoda pillar is five storeys high and each storey is divided into five panels, each with sculpted eaves and dougong brackets. In each panel is a niche housing a lifelike Buddhist statue. The walls, too, are carved with Buddhist pagodas in relievo, and pagodas with a stupa spire or storeyed tower can also be seen, all realistically moulded. (Photo by Sun Dazhong)

Cave No. 20 of the Yungang Grottoes, Datong, Shanxi

The Yungang Grottoes were first excavated in the 1st year of the reign of Heping (460), Emperor Wencheng of the Northern Wei Dynasty. The whole complex took more than 30 years to complete. Many of the caves also contain carved images of various architectural styles, perfect for studying the artistic modes of the Northern Wei Dynasty. Of these, Cave Nos. 16-20 are excavations of the early period. Also known as the 'five Tanyao caves,' their plans are elliptical and all serve to display statues of breathtaking dimension. Depicted here is Cave No. 20 of the Yungang Grottoes, an excellent example of the art of sculpture in Yungang. The front wall of the cave has collapsed, exposing the statue, but from the waist upwards, the giant buddha is well-preserved. The style is typical of the Northern Wei Dynasty, the statue expressive in form, the folds of the robe boldly delineated as are the relief sculptures of flying fairies and Buddhist images on the wall behind. Smiling gently, the Buddha expresses great dignity.

Hanging Monastery, Hunyuan, Shanxi / next page

The Hanging Monastery hugs the precipice above the gorge of Mt. Hengshan, and is where Buddhism, Taoism and Confucianism are practised. Built in the Northern Wei Dynasty, most of the buildings still in existence were renovated and reconstructed during the Qing Dynasty. It now comprises more than 30 Buddhist buildings the most attractive being the two towers connected by a wooden bridge clinging to the sheer precipice above the gorge. Its architecture naturally differs greatly from that of the traditional monastery in China, each storey being supported by wooden beams thrust into the cliff face. Records relate that all the structural members were made by the craftsmen in advance, then transported to the top of the mountain and lowered down together with the men, who were faced with the supremely difficult task of working suspended in mid-air.

Pagoda in the Songyue Monastery, Dengfeng, Henan

Located at the foot of Mt. Songshan, the Songyue Monastery originally served as a temporary residence for the emperors of the Northern Wei Dynasty. It became a monastery in the first year of the reign of Zhengguang (520), Emperor Xiaoming of the Northern Wei Dynasty, and called the Xianju (leading a quiet life) Monastery. It was renamed Songyue in the 2nd year of the reign of Renshou (620), Emperor Yangdi of the Sui Dynasty. Of the former monastery with its extensive courtyards, only the brick pagoda, built in the 4th year of Zhengguang is still extant. The pagoda is the earliest brick pagoda still in existence. 40 m high, with 12 sides and close eaves, it is unique. The first and second storeys share an archway on the four frontal sides, the other eight have more or less been left plain. The remaining 15 storeys have niches as a decorative element and corner pillars. The building tapers elegantly upwards, its eaves set gradually closer, creating a wonderful curved effect.

Pagoda in the Youguo Monastery, Kaifeng, Henan / opposite page

The pagoda was built in the first year of the reign of Huangyou (1049), Emperor Renzong of the Northern Song Dynasty. It was originally an octagonal wooden pagoda of 13 storeys but was later destroyed by lightning and an imperial edict issued for a glazed brick pagoda to be built on the same site. As glazed dark brown brick was used, the pagoda has come to be called the 'iron pagoda'. The octagonal plan of the original wooden pagoda was adopted and the building has thirteen storeys and is 54.66 m high. Its base now lies underground due to the silting up of the Yellow River. Access is through a door on the northern side and stairs integrated into the outside wall and the pagoda pillar in the centre spiral upwards, an arched doorway installed on each storey to provide adequate lighting. In appearance the pagoda is almost slender, but its firm structure has enabled it to withstand earthquakes and exposure to wind and rain for nearly one thousand years.

Pagoda Forest in the Shaolin Monastery, Dengfeng, Henan / preceding page

The pagoda forest is a graveyard for Buddhist monks. The one here represents the most extensive group of pagodas in China, consisting of more than 30 grave pagodas and dating from the Tang to the Qing dynasties. Built in the 19th year of the reign of Taihe (495), Emperor Xiaowen of the Northern Wei Dynasty, the Shaolin Monastery was for Indian monks. Later, it became the ancestral court of the Chan Sect and known throughout the world for the martial art of its monks. The grave pagodas are mostly brick-made, stone pagodas being few and far between. Generally, they are of seven storeys. About 15 m high, their styles are many and vary greatly in shape. Through them one can trace the development of brick and stone architecture of the various periods of ancient China, the pagoda for the elder Buddhist monk Fawan of the Tang Dynasty, the ordinary pagoda of the Song Dynasty, the pagoda for the Buddhist elder Yangong of the Jin Dynasty and the pagoda for the Buddhist elder Zhugong being particularly good examples.

Detail of the Xuan Zhuang Pagoda in the Xingjiao Monastery, Chang'an, Shanxi

Constructed in the 2nd year of the reign of Zongzhang (669), Emperor Gaozong of the Tang Dynasty, the grave pagoda in the Xingjiao Monastery was built for the eminent Tang Buddhist pilgrim Xuan Zhuang. Located in the western courtyard of the Xingjiao Monastery, it is 21 m high and square in plan. With a base side length of 5.2 m, it is here a five-storeyed tower pagoda. It is also the earliest tower-like brick pagoda still in existence in China. The first storey was renovated by later generations and the outer wall was changed into a simple and smooth brick wall. Higher up, its four storeys taper storey by storey. Octagonal tower-like columns divide each storey into three bays with lintels and on top of the columns are brick dougong brackets. Sandwiched between neighbouring storeys are projecting eaves with an iron bell hanging at the four corners. The Xuan Zhuang grave pagoda has tasteful simplicity, the necessary renovations sensitively undertaken.

Wei'e Precious Hall in the Wannian Monastery, Mount Emei, Emei, Sichuan

The Wannian (ten thousnd years) Monastery is the principal one of the six old monasteries on Mount Emei. First built in the Jin Dynasty, it was given the name of the White Water Monastery. During the Song Dynasty, it was known as the White Water Samantabhadra Monastery. During the reign of Wanli, Emperor Shenzong of the Ming Dynasty, it was officially named the Sacred Wannian Monastery on imperial orders. Formerly, it had seven halls. Today only the Brick Hall, the Lofty Precious Hall and the Hall of the Great Hero remain. The Lofty Precious Hall is situated behind the Brick Hall. A pool spanned by a stone bridge stretches out in front of the two-storeyed building, which has a corridor bordered by elegant wooden balusters running round its upper storey. The five bays are wider than usual, especially the central one, and as result two extra vertical columns have been installed. The single-eaved, palace-like roof has a gentle slope and together with the simple grey, brown and white colour scheme of the hall and the lack of ornamentation, the whole has been given a stately, gracious look. A statue of Amitaba Buddha is enshrined in the centre of the building with a statue of the god Weituo behind it.

Brick Hall of the Wannian Monastery on Mount Emei, Emei, Sichuan

The Brick Hall, the principal Buddhist building in the Wannian Monastery, was built during the reign of Wanli (1570-1620), Emperor Shenzong of the Ming Dynasty. The hall is 16 m high and it is square in plan with a base length of 15.6 m. A beamless structure, the semi-circular vaulted roof is supported by thick and solid brick walls from four sides. The Brick Hall has arched doorways on the south and north sides, and has ornamental dougong brackets, vertical and horizontal pillars as well as decorative windows on the outside walls, wooden structure in style. On the top of the roof and at the four corners stand five small stupas, together with two pairs of auspicious animals. Such buildings are for the worship and enshrinement of Tathagata Buddha. It is said that the Brick Hall formerly had a wooden structure and tiled roofing, but it was later destroyed by fire.

Bronze Statue of the Bodhisattva Samanthabhadra in the Wannian Monastery on Mount Emei, Emei, Sichuan

Mount Emei was where Bodhisattva Samanthabhadra performed Buddhist rites. Here it is Bodhisattva Samanthabhadra who is mainly worshipped and enshrined. The Bodhisattva Samanthabhadra enshrined in the Brick Hall of the Wannian Monastery rides on a white elephant. Cast in the 5th year of the reign of Taiping Xingguo (980), Emperor Taizong of the Northern Song Dynasty, the majestic elephant with its six tusks is 3.3 m high and was first cast in Chengdu in several parts that were then transported to the monastery and welded together. The Bodhisattva riding the elephant wears a wonderfully intricate gold crown with five Buddhas artistically incorporated, and Kasay robes, the folds made to drape realistically over her body. In her hands is an S-shaped ornamental rod of jade, symbolizing fortune.

Upper Part and Spire of the Pagoda in the Longhua Monastery, Shanghai
opposite page

The Longhua Monastery was reputedly first built in the 10th year of the reign of Chiwu (247) of Wu, the Three Kingdoms. It was rebuilt during the reign of Guangxu, Emperor Dezong of the Qing Dynasty, and given three Buddhist buildings as well as, for instance, the Abbot Tower Bell and the Drum Tower. Located directly south of the temple gate, the Longhua Monastery was reconstructed by Qian Hongshu, former King of Wu and Yue in the 2nd year of the reign of Taiping Xingguo (977), Emperor Taizong of the Northern Song Dynasty. It underwent renovation during successive dynasties, but style and features remained unchanged. The plan of the pagoda body is octagonal. About 40.4 m high, it is a seven-storeyed brick pagoda with wooden eaves. One of the oldest buildings in Shanghai, the pagoda has a square brick wooden-floored chamber in the centre of each floor. These chambers are turned 45 degrees as the pagoda climbs upwards and windows have been installed on the same four sides alternately. Song-style railings run round each floor and at each corner the eaves turn dramatically upwards, which, together with the tall and elegant spire, give the pagoda a light and lively appearance.

Beamless Hall in the Linggu Monastery, Nanjing, Jiangsu

The Linggu Monastery is located on the southern slope of Mt. Zhongshan. Its predecessor, the Kaishan Monastery, was built at Dulongfu, south of the mountain, in the 13th year of the reign of Tianjian (514) of the Liang Dynasty. It was moved to the present site and renamed the Linggu Monastery in the 14th year of the reign of Hongwu (1381), Emperor Taizu of the Ming Dynasty, when the Xiaoling tomb was built at Dulongfu. The monastery includes the Pool Freeing Captive Animals, the Diamond Hall, the Hall of the Heavenly King, the Beamless Hall, the Pilu Hall, Guanyin Tower, the Meditation Hall, guest rooms and miscellaneous buildings. This extensive monastery was destroyed in war, and of the original Ming Dynasty buildings only the Pool Freeing Captive Animals and the beamless hall have survived. The famous brick-built hall is five bays wide, extending an impressive 53.8 m from east to west. It is a double-eaved building with sloping roofing, and three elegantly moulded arched doorways and two windows grace the front. In addition to zoomorphic animals, the ridge has been given three stupas.

Interior View of the Beamless Hall in the Linggu Monastery, Nanjing, Jiangsu

Built of brick, the beamless hall has an arched structure, its name deriving from the fact that it is not timbered. Arched doors and windows piece the outer wall of the building, in perfect harmony with the dougong brackets and eave rim. Plain and simple in design, the hall is 22 m high, three bays deep and 38.75 m wide. Composed of three longitudinal arches, the front and rear two spans are rather short, the one in the middle having the biggest span, 11.25 m. Two arched windows are installed at the east and west ends. The picture shows the first narrow span to be seen on the southern side after entering the hall. Sunshine flooding in adds to the mysterious and solemn atmosphere of the huge vaulted building.

Eave Corner Decoration in the Hall of the Heavenly King of the Puji Monastery, Ningbo, Zhejiang

The Puji Monastery is situated at the foot of the Lingjiu Peak, south of Baihuading on Putuo. It is the principal monastery enshrining Guanyin Bodhisattva. The Buddhist building has seven courtyards, deep and open. The temple gate of the monastery is the only one of the Chinese temple gates to be closed throughout the year. Hence the local saying, "the temple gate of the front monastery never opens." The first Buddhist building one comes to is the Hall of the Heavenly King laid out in the traditional Buddhist monastery manner. Maitreya Buddha is enshrined directly in the centre of the hall, flanked by the Four Heavenly Kings. A statue of the god Weituo stands behind. First built in the 6th year of the reign of Wanli (1578), Emperor Shenzong of the Ming Dynasty, the hall was rebuilt in the 30th year of the reign of Kangxi (1691), Emperor Shengzu of the Qing Dynasty. Five bays wide, it is double-eaved with sloped roofing covered with yellow glazed titles. The eaves curve dramatically upwards at the corners, giving the whole a light and wonderfully artistic impression.

Ridge Decoration of the Precious Hall of the Great Hero in the Huiji Monastery on Mount Putuo, Ningbo, Zhejiang

Located at the col of Pusading, the highest peak of Mt. Foding, the Huiji Monastery is one of the three principal monasteries on the Putuo Mountain. The Precious Hall of the Great Hero is the principal Buddhist building in the monastery, in which the statue of Sakyamuni, Buddhist patriarch, is worshipped and enshrined. The great hall has five bays and is 23.3 m wide. It is single-eaved with its sloped roofing covered with yellow glazed tiles. The ridges are high and the zoomorphic animals are all in dragon-form. In ancient times dragons were regarded as symbol of imperial power. Such dragon ornaments are often to be found in monasteries on Putuo, not only indicating their imperial status but also that Putuo is an island, and the dragon the king of the sea.

Interior View of Yuantong Hall in the Puji Monastery, Ningbo, Zhejiang

Built upon the orders of Emperors Kangxi and Yongzheng of the Qing Dynasty, Yuantong Hall is the main hall for Guanyin Bodnisattva. Of wooden structure, it is five bays deep, about 24 m wide and 20 m high. Positioned right in the middle of the hall is a statue of Pilu Bodnisattva, 6.5 m high. The lotus throne it is sitting on is 2.3 m high. The Bodhisattva wears a solemn and kindly expression and is flanked by statues of Shancai and Longnu . Around the great hall 32 incarnations of bodhisattva are enshrined. Of these, some depict the old Buddha, some young Buddhist monks and nuns. Others are statues with superhuman powers or invisible might all helping to relieve living creatures of their suffering. The interior of the great hall is generous, its atmosphere highly spiritual.

Caisson Ceiling of Yubei Hall in the Puji Monastery, Ningbo, Zhejiang

The Puji Monastery can boast many a splendid building including the temple gate, the Hall of the Heavenly King, the Ghalan Hall, the Founder Hall, the Dharma Hall, the Hall of Arhat, the Hall of Cloud and Water, the Tower of the White Cloud and the Hall of Moonlight. Yubei Hall is the temple gate of the monastery. Five bays wide, it is double-eaved with sloped roofing. Though a temple gate, it differs from those of other old and large monasteries in that it is usually kept closed. Pilgrims enter the monastery through the side doors to the east and west. Only when grand ceremonies are held can pilgrims enter the monastery through the temple gate. In the middle of the hall is an imperial horizantal tablet bestowed by Emperor Kangxi. Yubei Hall is 16.1 m wide and 9.7 m deep. The inner part has a magnificent caisson ceiling decorated with layers of dougong brackets. A coiling dragon can clearly be seen in the carved centrepiece.

Haiyin Pool in the Puji Monastery on Mt.Putuo, Ningbo, Zhejiang

Also known as Mount Putuo Luojia, here is the place where Guanyin Bodhisattva performed Buddhist rites on one of the four famous Buddhist mountains. Also called the "Front Monastery," it represents one of the three principal monasteries on Putuo. It was the first important monastery for the Chan Sect, built under the supervision of the Law Master Xingzhu of the Ming Dynasty. Haiyin pool extends over an area of more than 10 mu and is used for lotus growing and freeing captive animals. It is spanned by three stone bridges: the one in the west called Yaochi (jasper lake) Bridge, the eastern one, Yongshou (longivity) Bridge, an arched bridge built in the 34th year of the reign of Wanli (1606), Emperor Shenzong of the Ming Dynasty, and the bridge in the middle facing Yubei Hall, the temple gate of the Puji Monastery. An octagonal pavilion stands on the latter bridge. The water in Haiyin pool is crystal clear and as smooth as mirror. It is an ideal place for pilgrims to stroll, with the pool as the focal point surrounded by lush and verdant vegetation.

Unwilling-to-Leave Guanyin Monastery on Mt. Putuo, Ningbo, Zhejiang

Putuo is a small and narrow island running from north to south, 80 km across the sea from the city of Ningbo. It is said that in the Tang Dynasty a Buddhist monk personally witnessed an incarnation of Guanyin expounding Buddhist teachings. From then on, Putuo became the place where Guanyin performed Buddhist rites. In the 12th year of the reign of Dazhong (858), Emperor Xuanzong of the Tang Dynasty, the Japanese Buddhist monk Aya Hanafusa came to Mt. Wutai to pay his respects to the Buddha and was given a statue of Guanyin. He planned to return to Japan by sea from Mingzhou (now Ningbo), but when passing Putuo island, his boat was hampered by hundreds of iron lotus flowers suddenly emerging out of the sea, and he was prevented from leaving. He then carried the Guanyin statue ashore and left it at the Kaiyuan Monastery, now the Unwilling-to-Leave Guanyin Monastery above Chaoyin cave. Located at the southeast corner of the island, the monastery faces Luojiashan island across the water.

Babao Ruyi Pagodas in the Ta'er Monastery, Huangzhong, Qinghai

There are more than 10 pagodas in the Ta'er Monastery, at the main entrance of which is an overhead pagoda, spanning a lane. Behind the Lesser Gold Tile Hall is a row of eight pagodas, known as the Babao Ruyi (eight treasures and good luck) pagodas as well as the silver pagoda in memory of Zong Khaba. To be seen here are the Babao Ruyi pagodas. Located in front of the Hall of the Dharma Protection God and the Living Buddha's administrative office, they were built in the 41st year of the reign of Qianlong (1776), Emperor Gaozong of the Qing Dynasty. A series of pagodas, neatly arranged in a row, symbolizes Sakyamini Buddha's 'eight right ways to attain Buddhahood.' These pagodas, in the form of an Indian stupa, comprise a large base, a square Sumeru throne narrowing in the middle, the pagoda body, the Wheel of the Law and a canopy and spire.

Tantra College in the Ta'er Monastery, Huangzhong, Qinghai

Built in memory of the founder of the Yellow Sect, Zong Khaba, the Ta'er Monastery is one of the six big monasteries of the Lamaist Gelupa (Yellow Sect). Huangzhong was the birthplace of Zong Khaba and Buddhist followers of later generations began to build the monastery there in his memory. It took 400 years to complete, and eventually covered an area of 40 ha. Laid out freely according to the topographical features of the mountain, the monastery principally consists of the Memorial Pagoda (Greater Gold Tile Hall), the Hall of the Dharma Protection God (Lesser Gold Tile Hall), the Greater Scripture Hall, four scripture colleges, the Living Buddha's administrative office and monks' residences. Tantra College is where Lamas customarily perform religious ceremonies. It is a Tibetan-style building with a flat roof and traditional ladder-shaped windows. Sitting on top of the roof is a gold, pavilion-like structure with a four-sided sloping roof. Over the entrance is a canopy with an ornate Han-style roof.

Caisson Ceiling of Tantra College in the Ta'er Monastery, Huangzhong, Qinghai

The Sera Monastery, Zhebang Monastery, Zhashilunpu Monastery, Labuleng Monastery, Ta'er Monastery and Gandan Monastery that no longer exists are the six big monasteries of the Buddhist Yellow Sect. It was above all in the Ta'er Monastery that the traditional architecture of the Han and Hui was adopted. The buildings follow the mountain valley and Tantra College is located at the end of the valley, completing the whole group of buildings. The monastery is an excellent example of the successful integration of Han and Tibetan details into its architecture, the skills of Huangnan wood- and Hezhou brick carving both prominent. Illustrated here is a detail of the caisson ceiling in Tantra College presenting an exquisite and rare depiction of Lamaist architectural layout and Buddhist instruments.

Close Shot of Potala Palace Viewed from the North, Lhasa, Tibet

At the foot of the Red Mountain, behind Potala Palace, there was a beautiful stretch of water called the Pool of the Dragon King. It was low-lying land, left after excavations had taken place for the construction of Potala Palace. After renovations by Dalai VI, it was used for the Palace of the Dragon King. Potala Palace is 360 m wide from east to west and 119 m high. The lofty tower has majestic dignity and is the spiritual symbol of the Tibetan people. Its outer wall is faced with coloured stone. The different facades taper dramatically upwards and the interior is of beam and pillar construction. The windows, installed towards the top, have the typical Tibetan ladder-form. Emerging as it does from the rocks of the mountain, the palace has a solid and powerful appearance and is an outstanding example of the talent of Tibetan architects.

Gold Tops of the Red Palace in Potala Palace, Lhasa, Tibet

The Red Palace contains mainly halls for the soul pagodas of past generations and various Buddhist halls for worship. The Soul Pagoda of the Dalai consists of three parts, the pagoda base, bottle and top. The treated corpse of the Dalai was kept in the pagoda bottle. The body of the pagoda was decorated with gold leaf and inlaid with jade, making the whole extremely sumptuous. At the highest point of the Red Palace are seven gold roof-top structures, covering the few principal Buddhist halls and the Hall of the Soul Pagoda. These structures take the form of sloped roofing, with the central ridge in gold, its decorative figures like those of the eave corners moulded in bronze and plated with gold. The gold glitters in the sunlight adding resplendence to the mightiness of the famous palace.

Hall of Sunshine in Potala Palace, Lhasa, Tibet

The White Palace is where the Dalai handles political affairs and resides. A palace of seven storeys, its principal hall is the Eastern Great Hall on the fourth storey. From the Great Hall upward, each storey has a small yard accessed by winding corridors. The Dalai's living quarters are on the top floor, and called the Hall of Sunshine on account of the sunny location. From up here a bird's-eye view is to be had of the whole of Lhasa. The Hall of Sunshine is divided into two. The western hall served as the residence of Dalai XIII, the eastern part Dalai XIV's, including sleeping quarters, the room for studying the scriptures, rest room etc. Mural paintings on Buddhist themes cover the walls, richly carved furniture and heavy carpets fill the rooms, brightly coloured curtains hang at the windows, the atmosphere pervading the rooms one of peace.

Cuoqin Great Hall in the Zhebang Monastery, Lhasa, Tibet / preceding page

With its quota of 7,700 lamas, the Zhebang Monastery is the largest of the three big monasteries in Tibet. It was constructed under the supervision of Jiangyang Quejie,a disciple of the Gelupa Sect founder Zong Khaba in the 14th year of the reign of Yongle (1416), Emperor Chengzu of the Ming Dynasty. Cuoqin Great Hall is the highest administrative building, the place where the whole monastery gathers together. It is also the largest scripture hall of the monastery. Covering 2,000 m^2, its portico is 7 bays wide. The hall, with its 183 columns, can accommodate 9,000 lamas for the chanting of scriptures. The scripture hall is square in plan. It is three storeys high and a central caisson ceiling allows light to penetrate. It has the typical form of a scripture hall in a Tibetan lamasery.

Portico of Cuoqin Great Hall in the Zhebang Monastery, Lhasa, Tibet

The white buildings of the monastery straggle up the slopes of Mt. Gengbeiwuzi in the western suburbs of Lhasa and give the monastery its picturesque name (Zhebang meaning heap of rice in Tibetan). Of all the Buddhist buildings, the Cuoqin Great Hall is the most magnificent, its layout dictated by the requirements of the scripture rotation ceremonies. A small courtyard is surrounded by the entrance hall, scripture hall and the Hall of Buddha. The portico leading to the entrance to the Great Hall has impressive carved pillars, painted an eye-catching red. These, together with the blue purlins and the intricately carved brackets, give prominence to the main entrance.

The White Palace Portico of Potala Palace, Lhasa, Tibet / opposite page

The White Palace is to be found in the eastern half of Potala Palace. The Hall of Sunshine, the highest building in the White Palace, represents the living quarters of the Dalai, and includes a scripture hall, a parlour, a room for studying the scriptures and sleeping quarters. A long winding path takes one upwards from the foot of the mountain to the Pengcuduolang gate leading to the White Palace, in front of which is a courtyard enclosed by a two-storeyed winding corridor. Steep wooden staircases take one from here to the magnificent portico. Its wooden pillars, main entrance, door leaves, dougong brackets and the lintel are all embellished with gloriously rich carvings and paintings, the dominant colour being red. The White Palace represents the Tibetan architectural style at its most glorious.

Detail of the Greater Bodhi Pagoda in the Baiju Monastery, Jiangzi, Tibet
opposite page

The Greater Bodhi Pagoda was built in the 12th year of the reign of Yongle (1414), Emperor Chengzu of the Ming Dynasty. It took 10 years to complete. The plan of the pagoda bottle is circular with a diameter of 20 m. Both the pagoda bottle and base are earthen constructions. On top of the pagoda, the cup forms a hollow room. A watchful pair of Buddhist eyes can be seen painted over the doorways on the four sides of the pagoda cup that in design resembles the Nepalese Buddhist pagoda. The conical Wheel of the Law has bronze cladding gilded with gold, its interior consisting of two hollow chambers one above the other. The pagoda culminates in a five-metre high spire with the same cladding as the Wheel of the Law. The entire pagoda has 108 doorways, 76 niches and over 1, 000 Buddhist statues of various kinds. Inside the chambers, the walls are finely painted with murals depicting Buddhist themes.

The Greater Bodhi Pagoda in the Baiju Monastery, Jiangzi, Tibet

Built in the centre of a group of monastic buildings, the Greater Bodhi Pagoda (in Tibetan, ban gen que dian) of the Baiju Monastery is the finest of the Tibetan pagodas. 40 m high, it is composed of four parts: the pagoda base, pagoda bottle, pagoda cup and Wheel of the Law. Covering an area of 2,200 m², its tapering base has five storeys, each with 20 right-angled corners. The polygonal composition of the pagodas is very precise, the oblique lines of the architecture running north-south and east-west, basically forming an equilateral triangle with the base and resulting in a proportionally satisfying building. Also known as the 'pagoda of pagodas,' it is a stately, awe-inspiring building, the crystallization of various pagodas.

Hall of the Soul Pagoda for Panchen IV in Zhashilunpu Monastery, Xikazi, Tibet
opposite page

The Zhashilunpu Monastery was built by Gendun Zhuba, a disciple of Zong Khaba, in the 12th year of the reign of Zhengdong (1447), Emperor Yingzong of the Ming Dynasty. In the 8th year of the reign of Wanli (1600), Emperor Shengzong of the Ming Dynasty, it became the residence of Panchen IV and Panchens of later generations. Like Cuoqin Great Hall, it also has four Zhacangs and more than 60 Kangcun villages. Situated halfway up the mountain, northeast of the monastery, there is another 35-metre high platform for exhibiting the Buddha. During important religious festivals, the platform has a huge statue of Buddha displayed on it for Buddhist followers to pay their respects. In the monastery there are another six halls containing soul pagodas, where the remains of Panchen Lamas are kept. The pagoda body is clad with silver pieces inlaid with precious stones. The hall has a spectacular roof tiled in gold that glitters in the sun.

Scripture Rotation Corridor in the Southern Sajia Monastery, Sajia, Tibet

The Sajia Monastery is the principal monastery of the Lamaist Sajia Sect in Tibet. It was originally divided into the southern and northern monasteries, but now only the southern one remains. Seen here is the scripture rotation corridor in the Southern Sajia Monastery. The scripture rotation drums are lined up along the corridor wall. The larger ones are anchored in a frame and can be rotated manually by believers. The six words, "Ah, Ma, Ni, Ba, Mi, Hong," the origin of all Buddhist scriptures, are carved on the drums, which are to be found in many a Tibetan Buddhist monastery. The Sajia Monastery also houses a rare collection of Jialongma scriptures in addition to other relics of great historic and cultural value.

General View of the Southern Sajia Monastery, Sajia, Tibet

In the 11th century A.D., with the Kuns family as centre, the Sajia Sect (commonly known as the 'floral sect') of Tibetan Buddhism was created. In the mid-13th century, Basba, leader of the Sajia Sect, was granted the title of State Master of the Yuan Dynasty. In the 4th year of the reign of Xianchun (1268), Emperor Duzong of the Yuan Dynasty, the Southern Sajia Monastery was established on the plain by the Chongqu River. Not only centre of a religious sect but also of regional political power, the monastery was built as a fortified castle, its form typical of Yuan Dynasty castles with double rectangular walls, watchtower at the four corners and centre of the outer earthern wall, patrolled by soldiers, and an 8 m wide moat. The inner, 3 m thick wall is of rammed earth and stone and rises to an impressive 9 m, the length of the outer side walls being 210 m. Within the walls are the great scripture hall, the Buddhist hall, living quarters for the monks and the regional administrative office of Basba.

Pagoda in the Chongsheng Monastery, Dali, Yunnan

The Chongsheng Monastery was located on the banks of Lake Erhai. The monastery buildings no longer exist, but three pagodas have remained intact, the principal one being the Qianxun Pagoda. Built after the reign of Kaiyuan, Emperor Xianzong of the Tang Dynasty, it was renovated in later dynasties. Rising to a height of 70 m, the pagoda stands on a two-storeyed base with stone banisters. Square in plan, it has 16 storeys of close-eaves with the 16-storeyed interior a hollow cylindrical shape. Structurally it belongs to the category of the close-eaved pagoda of the Tang Dynasty, and is similar in structure to the Lesser Wild Goose Pagoda in Xi'an. The pagoda, with its elegant, mildly tapering form is a fine Tang close-eaved building, 16 storeys of close-eaves a rare sight. Two towering ten-storeyed, close-eaved Song pagodas stand to its north and south-west, the three together resembling the legs of a tripod.

Diamond Throne Pagoda in the Cideng Monastery, Huhhot, Inner Mongolia
opposite page

The Diamond Throne Pagoda is the last building one comes to in the courtyard of the Cideng Monastery. Built in the 5th year of the reign of Yongzheng (1727), Emperor Shizong of the Qing Dynasty, it is an imitation of the style of the Diamond Throne Pagoda in the Greater Zhengjue Monastery in Beijing. A brick structure, the pagoda is 16.5 m high and the exterior walls of the base have seven storeys of short, projecting eaves. Sutras in Mongolian, Tibetan and Sanskrit are inscribed below the first-storey eave. Above the base are the imperial throne and pagodas. The outer walls of the base and body of the pagoda are decorated with lion, peacock, Wheel of the Law, treasure bottle and other motifs frequently used on Lamaist buildings. Yellow and green glazed titles decorate the space below each eave of the pagoda base as well as the throne, each tile with a Buddhist statue in relievo. A huge archway, over which a tablet hangs bearing the words, "Diamond Throne Relic Pagoda" in Mongolian, Tibetan and Chinese, is set into the south wall of the diamond throne.

Street Scene in a Kangcun Village of the Zhebang Monastery, Lhasa, Tibet

In addition to the Cuoqin Great Hall, the Zhebang Monastery also has four Zhacangs (Institutes for lamas to study the scriptures) and scores of Kangcun villages, providing accommodation for lamas of different ethnic origin. Sangluo Kangcun is, for instance, for the lamas from Mongolia, Hamudong Kangcun for those from the Qinghai region, Luoba Kangcun for those from Sichuan. The Zhebang Monastery resembles a religious city with its thousands of monks organized within a rigidly stratified system. As a result, there has been continual expansion, meaning that there is no unified plan. Buddhist houses straggle up the mountain-side, arranged along streets and lanes, following stone steps upwards. Such a layout differentiates it entirely from that of Buddhist monasteries on Han territory.

Thousand-Buddha Cave in Bozikelic, Turpan, Xinjiang

The original meaning of Bozikelic is "Home of Decoration," and formerly it served as a stone cave monastery for Buddhist monks performing Buddhist rites in seclusion. The cave is 45 km northeast of Tupan along the river valley of Murtok at the northern foot of Mt. Flaming. The cliff is riddled with over 50 stone caves big and small. Some are Chaitya caves for enshrining and worshipping Buddhist statues. Others are Pikeluo caves for monks practising Buddhism. Both types were excavated during the period from the Northern and Southern Dynasties to that of the Yuan. Statues and murals depicting the life of Buddha and Buddhist themes in general formerly decorated the caves and were an excellent source of reference for the study of the Gaochang culture. Unfortunately, they suffered greatly at the hands of foreign exploiters at the beginning of the 20th century and today only hollow Buddhist niches and faint traces of the murals are to be seen.

Illustrated Dougong Bracket, Inner Lintel and Square Pillar

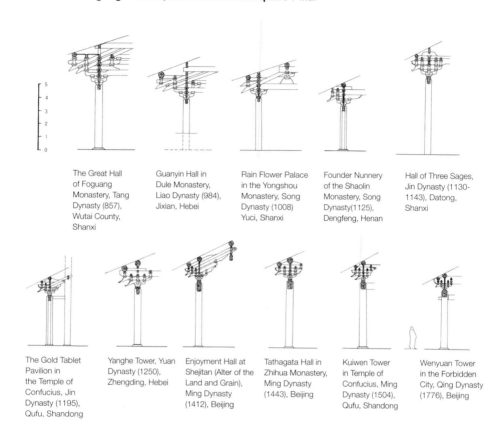

The Great Hall of Foguang Monastery, Tang Dynasty (857), Wutai County, Shanxi

Guanyin Hall in Dule Monastery, Liao Dynasty (984), Jixian, Hebei

Rain Flower Palace in the Yongshou Monastery, Song Dynasty (1008) Yuci, Shanxi

Founder Nunnery of the Shaolin Monastery, Song Dynasty(1125), Dengfeng, Henan

Hall of Three Sages, Jin Dynasty (1130-1143), Datong, Shanxi

The Gold Tablet Pavilion in the Temple of Confucius, Jin Dynasty (1195), Qufu, Shandong

Yanghe Tower, Yuan Dynasty (1250), Zhengding, Hebei

Enjoyment Hall at Shejitan (Alter of the Land and Grain), Ming Dynasty (1412), Beijing

Tathagata Hall in Zhihua Monastery, Ming Dynasty (1443), Beijing

Kuiwen Tower in Temple of Confucius, Ming Dynasty (1504), Qufu, Shandong

Wenyuan Tower in the Forbidden City, Qing Dynasty (1776), Beijing

Drawings of the Dougong Bracket in Past Dynasties

The dougong bracket is a component member used between column caps, lintel pillars, house-eaves or structures. In "*A Treatise on Architectural Methods*" written during the Song Dynasty, it was called puzuo. In "*Construction Methods*" appearing during the Qing Dynasty, it was called douke, but it was also referred to as dougong. During the Tang and Song dynasties, it was integrated into the beam and square pillar. In addition to allowing more depth to be given to the eaves, it also became a structural unit integrating the whole wooden structure. After the Ming and Qing dynasties, the structural function of the dougong degenerated and it became chiefly a decorative component placed between the pillar-net and the house-top structure. The dougong brackets of the Tang and Song dynasties were large and wonderfully ornate units, set close together, their height ranging from one-third to half that of the column. Those of the Ming and Qing dynasties were much shorter and smaller, their height about one-ninth to one-fifth that of the column, their function obviously much less important.

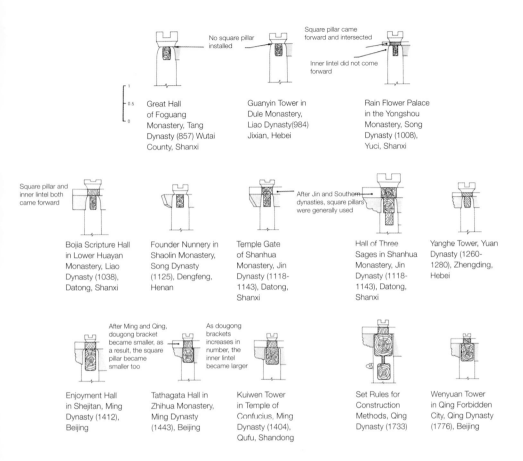

No square pillar installed

Square pillar came forward and intersected

Inner lintel did not come forward

1
0.5
0

Great Hall of Foguang Monastery, Tang Dynasty (857) Wutai County, Shanxi

Guanyin Tower in Dule Monastery, Liao Dynasty(984) Jixian, Hebei

Rain Flower Palace in the Yongshou Monastery, Song Dynasty (1008), Yuci, Shanxi

Square pillar and inner lintel both came forward

After Jin and Southern dynasties, square pillars were generally used

Bojia Scripture Hall in Lower Huayan Monastery, Liao Dynasty (1038), Datong, Shanxi

Founder Nunnery in Shaolin Monastery, Song Dynasty (1125), Dengfeng, Henan

Temple Gate of Shanhua Monastery, Jin Dynasty (1118-1143), Datong, Shanxi

Hall of Three Sages in Shanhua Monastery, Jin Dynasty (1118-1143), Datong, Shanxi

Yanghe Tower, Yuan Dynasty (1260-1280), Zhengding, Hebei

After Ming and Qing, dougong bracket became smaller, as a result, the square pillar became smaller too

As dougong brackets increases in number, the inner lintel became larger

Enjoyment Hall in Shejitan, Ming Dynasty (1412), Beijing

Tathagata Hall in Zhihua Monastery, Ming Dynasty (1443), Beijing

Kuiwen Tower in Temple of Confucius, Ming Dynasty (1404), Qufu, Shandong

Set Rules for Construction Methods, Qing Dynasty (1733)

Wenyuan Tower in Qing Forbidden City, Qing Dynasty (1776), Beijing

Drawings of the Inner Lintel and Square Pillar of Past Dynasties

The inner lintel (known as lan'e in the Qing Dynasty) is a component between eave columns. The square pillar (known as pingban fang in the Qing Dynasty) is a piece of horizontal timber placed on the inner lintel, forming a T-shaped section.

In the architecture of the Tang and early Liao dynasties, there was no square pillar to be seen, but it began to be used over the inner lintel up to the late Liao and Song dynasties. The inner lintel and squared pillar changed with the size of the dougong bracket, the inner lintel tending to become thick and bulky, and the square pillar reduced in size. Structurally, the two tended to become T-shaped during the Song, Jin and Yuan dynasties and up to the end of the Ming and Qing dynasties, the square pillar became smaller.

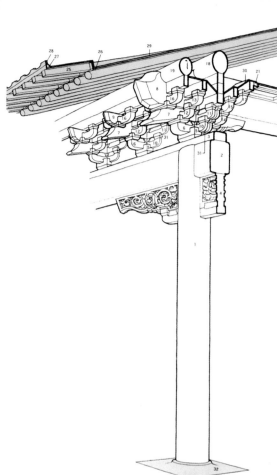

Illustrated Drawing of the Outer Eave Dougong Bracket of the Qing Dynasty

1. eave column 2. lintel rafter 3. flat board rafter 4. queti bracket 5. dou seat 6. uploading arm 7. cantilever arm 8. pointed beam-end 9. grasshopper head 10. the lowest longitudinal bracket arm 11. cross-shaped longitudinal bracket arm 12. outward-pulling longitudinal bracket arm 13. outward-pulling cross-shaped bracket arm 14. inward-pulling longitudinal bracket arm 15. inward-pulling cross-shaped bracket arm 16. outward-pulling side bracket arm 17. inward-pulling side bracket arm 18. eave purlin 19. purlin projecting eave 20. well-opening rafter 21. supporting beam 22. supporting piece 23. ceiling 24. eave rafter 25. flying rafter 26. inside opening piece 27. connecting eave 28. tile opening 29. roof boarding 30. bracket-covering board 31. bracket pad 32. column base

The Dougong Bracket Combination in the Ancient Architecture of China

The hierarchical system of Chinese feudal society meant that as far as architecture was concerned there were great differences in what materials and structures could be used for what buildings. The dougong structure, for instance, could only be installed on top of the columns and square pillars of the inner and outer eaves of palace buildings, monasteries and other important edifices. What was termed dougong in the Qing Dynasty was puzuo in the Song Dynasty. It was first used to support the beam head, square pillar cap and the weight of the outer eaves. Later, it was used to support the structure joint. The number of "tiers" also varied in each "pile," normally representing the extent to which the eaves protruded.

The chief structural members of the dougong bracket are dou, sheng, gong, qiao, ang, and fang. Dou means a piece of square wood in the form of a dou measure (with a bigger opening and a narrower bottom). Sheng, in shape, also looks like a dou measure, but is smaller in size. Gong is a rectangular piece of wood with its two ends curved giving it a bow-shaped appearance. The shape of qiao is more or less the same as that of gong, but because the force it receives is great, its section measurement is rather high. Ang is a straight and long structural member. Those used in the Ming and Qing dynasties were mostly false ones. The square pillar is a linking structural member that integrates each group of dougong. Of the dougong structural parts, dou is the total bearing point. A simple dougong bracket, such as one dou three shengs means the structure part of dou supporting gong, gong supporting sheng and sheng supporting dougong again. The concrete structure of each group of dougong generally consists of outer eave dougong under the eave, inner eave dougong in the room and plan seat dougong in the plan seat corridor. Their structure and scale are not exactly the same. Among them, the outer eave dougong is the most typical. (See illustration on the left)

Glossary

Baoxia (porch)
An extra small room in front of the entrance of
the principal building.

Cha (spire)
A decorative element at the top of a Buddhist
pagoda, also known as the Buddhist Wheel of the
Law.

Chaoshou huilang (folding-arms corridor)
A corridor designed in the form of folding arms.

Chongyan (double eaves)
House eaves of two or more tiers.

Chuan (rafter)
Timber on top of the purlin and forming a right
angle to it to support the roof boarding and the
roof. It can be square or round.

Chuangdong (window opening)
Openings in the form of windows in the wall but
without a casement.

Chuihua men (ornate gate)
Over the second gate of an old residence a vault or
arched roof was built embellished with sculptures
and known as 'guoting' (walk-through pavilion) or
'chuihua men'.

Cijian (next bay)
The part between the central and the concluding
bays.

Cuanjianding (tapering top)
Pyramidal roof of a building, it may be round,
square or polygonal in plan.

Cuidupo (stupa)
Originally a tomb for the dead, paved with brick
and earth. From outside it resembles a round
upturned cauldron. Later, it developed into a solid
building composed of platform, upturned alms
bowl, treasure box and Wheel of the Law.

Sengjialuomo
Also short for senggalan, and originally forming
the basis of a Buddhist residence. Later it was
used in the buildings in the country that became
Buddhist temples.

Daozuo (houses with a northern exposure)
Houses facing the main building on the central
axis, generally with northern exposure.

Dougong (dougong bracket)
A supporting bracket in traditional Chinese
wooden-structured architecture, composed of
a piece of timber in the form of a dou measure
and a piece of horizontal timber in the form of a
bow laid on top of one another. In early times, the
dougong was part of the wooden structural system.
After the Ming and Qing dynasties, its structural
function declined and it became chiefly decorative.

Fang (square pillar)
A subsidiary timber smaller than the beam usually
in the form of a square pillar.

Geshan (partition board)
An exquisitely sculptured structure that served to
divide indoor and outdoor space.

Guojieta (pagoda spanning a lane)
A pagoda built on a door mount spanning a lane to
allow pedestrians to pass through.

Huata (flower pagoda)
A single-eaved pagoda with a multitude of
Buddhist niches, statues of Buddha and sculptured
animals, all lending a floral effect.

Jin'gang baozuota (diamond-throne pagoda)
Its lower part consists of a huge base, known
as the 'diamond throne.' It is carved all round
with exquisite Buddhist statues and patterns. The
lower part has a door and on top are five small
pagodas, the central one slightly larger and used
for enshrining and worshipping the five principal
Buddhist relics of the tantric sect.

Huilang (winding corridor)
A winding covered corridor around a courtyard.

Jian (bay or space)
Bay or space between two pairs of pillars.

Jingshe (spiritual residence)
A Buddhist house originally used as a private
dwelling. Later, as more monks came to reside in
the monastery, large-scale residential quarters came
into existence.

Juzhe (rise and depression of roof)
The cross-section of a roof is composed of the
rise (the rise of the ridge rafters) and the fall (the
fall of the rafter line.) This allows for drainage and
light under the eave.

Jinshen (depth)
The distance between the front eave- and the rear
eave-columns of a building.

Lamata (dagoba)
Also known as the pagoda in the form of an
upturned alms bowl. The lower part of the dagoba
has a truncated tapering base on the top of which
is the section shaped like an upturned alms bowl.
Above this is the crown, composed of the Sumeru-
throne, the Wheel of the Law, the canopy and roof
crown.

Lan'gan (baluster)
Railing flanking a platform, staircase or corridor
and installed as a safety precaution.

Langwu (building and covered passageway)
Wing rooms on either side of the Buddhist hall
and the covered passageway.

**Langyuanshi simiao (corridor-style
monastery)**
A Buddhist pagoda stands in the centre of
the monastery and is surrounded by Buddhist
buildings.

Liuliwa (glazed tile)
Tiles coloured with glaze, mostly yellow or green,
blue, black and other colours. They are generally
used in palatial buildings and monasteries.

Lougeshita (tower-style pagoda)
There are two forms: the wooden version and
the brick and stone structure. The latter has an
inner lintel, door and window on each storey. The
interior has a staircase allowing visitors to have a
panoramic view of the surrounding countryside
from the top. It represents the typical Buddhist
pagoda in China.

Miankuan (width)
The distance between the columns in front of a
building. The length of the facade of a building is
also called miankuan.

Miyanta (close-eaved pagoda)
Generally, the first storey of the pagoda body is
especially high and provides an important surface
for decoration. Some are sculptured with statues
of Buddha and warriors, others with lotus flowers
and geometric patterns. Others can have doors,
windows and pillars. From the second storey
upwards, the pagoda eaves are piled up layer upon
layer without doors or windows. Most close-eaved
pagodas are solid and cannot be ascended.

Nu'erqiang (girl-wall)
A low wall built on a flat house-top, a high stage or
a city wall.

Paifang or Pailou (archway)
Originally it was a building of memorial nature praising the 'merits and virtues' of certain individuals in the locality. At the same time it was also used as a means of dividing and controlling space. Generally, they are built of timber, brick and stone, glazed material, etc.

Peidian (subordinate building)
The term describing buildings smaller in scale than the main hall of a palace or monastery and located on either side or in front of the same.

Pingwuding (flat house-top)
A house top with a drainage slope generally less than10% degrees.

Pikeluo
A kind of grotto in ancient India. Its plan may be square with little niches cut out on three sides for Buddhist monks to chant scriptures in or take a rest.

Puowuding (sloped roofing)
A house-top with a drainage slope generally in excess of 10% degrees.

Qingshui qiang (dry wall)
A brick wall that is not whitewashed or plastered. The crevices in the wall are filled with liquid cement or whitewashed. The outer appearance of the wall is neat, clean and unadorned. It is a kind of wall mostly used for the external wall. It is sometimes used in palatial buildings and monasteries.

Sanheyuan (triangle)
A living space composed of buildings on three sides and an enclosing wall.

Shanmen (temple gate)
The outer gate of a temple.

Shanqiang (gable)
Three-cornered part of an outside wall between the sloped roofing.

Shaojian (end bay)
The end sections on the left and right of a building.

Shoufen (shrinking part)
To make a building stand more steadily, the outer eave columns incline slightly inwards. The method is known as shoufen in Chinese or batter.

Siheyuan (quadrangle)
The traditional Chinese residence in the form of a courtyard, whereby buildings completely surround the yard , the base is enclosed by a wall and there are generally no windows facing the exterior.

Tacha (pagoda spire)
The topmost part of a pagoda, above the canopy.

Taji (pagoda base)
The foundation of the pagoda, including the base and the base seat (or throne).

Tashen (pagoda body)
The main part of a pagoda. It is the design of this section that determines into which category a given pagoda falls.

Tianjing (skylight, ceiling)
1) Open land or empty space enclosed by bulidings on four or three sides or by an enclosing wall. It also means a small opening to let in daylight from above, well-like in shape opening up to the sky, hence the name tianjing.
2) In ancient times, it meant the ceiling, also known as canopy or caisson ceiling.

Tianhua (ceiling)
A kind of ceiling with boarding protecting the area above the beams and crisscrossed with wooden strips.

Tinggeshita (pavilion-style pagoda)
Most are single-eaved and of simple structure. It can be square, hexagonal, octagonal and sometimes of other shapes. Generally, they are Buddhist monks' tomb pagodas.

Wumian (roofing)
The covering on the top of a building, including the surface and the supporting structures. The chief function of the former is to drain rain water away, the latter to support the surface form a slope and transfer the work load.

Wuliang dian (beamless hall)
Buddhist hall built solely of brick and stone, and usually arched. From the outside the style is similar to that of a timber building.

Xianglun (buddhist wheel of the law)
Decorative element on top of the Buddhist pagoda.

Xumi zuo (sumeru throne)
A kind of platform in traditional architecture, representing the "throne of Mt. Sumeru." Generally, it is paved with brick and stone.

Xiangfang (wing room)
Buildings in front and on the left and right of the main building.

Yan (eave)
part of the overhanging roof stretching to the wall or beyond the column.

Zhaobi (screen wall)
A screen wall facing the gate and just inside it to prevent strangers from peering in, also knwon as the yingbi.

Zaojing (caisson ceiling)
The elevated dome structure on the ceiling of a building.

Zhiti (chitya)
A kind of stone cave in ancient India. Its plan is U-shaped. In the middle and rear part is a stupa and the open space in the cave is used for religious ceremonies as well as the worshipping of a Buddhist patriarch.

Zhonggulou (bell and drum tower)
A joint name for a bell tower and a drum tower, it served to give the correct time in ancient China. Bell and drum towers are located on either side of the central axis inside the temple gate. Double-eaved and two-storeyed, they are generally square in plan.

Zhuchu (column base)
Carved out of stone, its height is roughly equal to the column diameter. In shape, it may be round like a drum, a section of a melon, a lotus flower petal, octagon and or given another shape. Its function is to prevent water seeping into the wood and the columns, as well as for artistic decoration.

Zhengfang (main house)
The principal building on the main central axis of a residence.

Chronology of Major Events in the History of Chinese Architecture

Christian era	Chinese Dynastic Years	Events or Achievements
The Neolithic Age		
ca. 4800 BC		Sites of ganlan buildings (pile-supported structures with wooden floor above the ground) of Hemudu Culture were unearthed in the northeast of Hemudu Village in Yuyao County, Zhejiang Province.
ca. 4500 BC		Sites of Various kinds of primitive houses of Yangshao Culture, including a big house square in plan were unearthed in Banpo Village near Xi'an, Shaanxi Province.
2310~2378 BC		A sacrificial altar of Liangzhu Culture was unearthed at Yaoshan in Yuhang County, Zhejiang Province.
ca. 3000 BC		Temple of Goddess of Hongshan Culture was discovered at Niuheliang in Lingyuan County, Liaoning Province.
The Shang Dynasty		
1900~1500 BC		An Early Shang site of a high-terrace palatial complex was unearthed at Erlitou Village in Yanshi County, Henan Province.
17th~11th c. BC		Rectangular houses with rammed earth foundations and walls were unearthed in present Zhengzhou, Henan Province.
1384 BC	15th year, Pangeng	Capital of the Shang was moved to Yin where the Late Shang capital was constructed, which was unearthed and referred to as the Yin Ruins at Xiaotun Village in Anyang, Henan Province.
The Western Zhou Dynasty		
1095 BC	10th year, Chengwang	An ancestral temple of the Zhou Court was unearthed at Fengchu Village in Qishan County, Shaanxi Province.
The Spring and Autumn Period		
475 BC	45th year, Jingwang	Rules for capital planning of the Zhou Court were recorded in the Survey on Construction Work collected in the Ritual of Zhou, in which it was regulated that the Ancestral Temple was to be located to the left of the palace, and the Altar of Land and Grain, to its right.
The Warring States Period		
350~207 BC		Site of Xianyang Palace of the Qin State, a high-terrace building complex, was unearthed at Xianyang, Shaanxi Province.
The Qin Dynasty		
221 BC	26th year, Shi Huang Di	The Qin conquered the six states and built palaces in styles to imitate those of the conquered states on the northern sloping fields of Xianyang. An army of 300,000 men, led by Meng Tian, was sent to drive out the northern nomadic Hun invasions and to build the Great Wall from Lintao (in present-day Gansu province) in the west to Liaodong (the east of present-day Liaoning Province) in the east. Capital Xianyang was constructed and extended.
221~210 BC	26th~37th years, Shi Huang Di	Construction of Shi Huang Di's mausoleum started in Lintong, Shaanxi Province.
212 BC	35th year, Shi Huang Di	Construction of the Epang (or Efanggong) Palace began on the south bank of the Wei River, Xianyang.
The Western Han Dynasty		
200 BC	7th year, Gaozu	Palatial city in Chang'an (present-day Xi'an) was under construction and Changle Palace (Palace of Everlasting Happiness) was erected.
199 BC	8th year, Gaozu	Construction of Wei Yang palace started. The Palace was completed in the next year.
140~87 BC	Reign period of Wudi	Construction of Maoling Tomb (the Mausoleum of Emperor Wudi) started in Xingping County, Shaanxi Province.
138 BC	4th year, Jianyuan, Wudi	Shang Lin Garden of the Qin was extended in a vast area of 300 li across with 70 detached palaces included.
127 BC	2nd year, Yuanshuo, Wudi	The Great Wall with watchtowers, passes and beacon towers was reconstructed. Later on, the Great wall underwent five large-scale reconstruction works.

Christian era	Chinese Dynastic Years	Events or Achievements
104 BC	1st year, Taichu, Wudi	Jian Zhang Palace was built in the western outskirts of Chang'an City.
101 BC	4th year, Taichu, Wudi	Ming Guang Palace was built in the City of Chang'an.
32 BC	1st year, Jianshi, Chengdi	Altars for offering sacrifices to God of Heaven and God of Earth were erected in the southern and northern suburbs of Chang'an respectively. Thereafter the locations of the Altar of Heaven and the Altar of Earth in the planning of the capital city were so established as a rule.
4 AD	4th year, Yuanshi, Pingdi	Mingtang, Biyong (halls for handling state affairs and promulgating politics as well as schooling) and Lingtai (Terrace of Spirit) were erected inside and outside Chang'an.
The Xin Dynasty		
20 AD	1st year, Dihuang, Wang Mang	More than ten palaces, including Jian Zhang Palace, were demolished. The disassembled materials were used to build eleven buildings in the southern suburbs of Chang'an, known as the Nine Temples of Wang Mang historically.
The Eastern Han Dynasty		
68 AD	11th year, Yongping, Mingdi	Baima Si (the Temple of White Horse) was erected in Luoyang.
Period of the Three Kingdoms		
220 AD	1st year, Huangchu, Wendi of the Wei	Cao Pi founded the Kingdom of Wei with its capital moved from Yecheng to Luoyang.
221 AD	1st year, Zhangwu, the Shu Han	Liu Bei founded the Kingdom of Shu Han, making Chengdu (in present-day Sichuan province) its capital.
229 AD	8th year, Huangwu, the Wu	Sun Quan moved the capital of the Kingdom of Wu from Wuchang to Jianye (present-day Nanjing). The capital city with the palace were then constructed.
235 AD	3rd year, Qinglong, Mingdi of the Wei	The Palace of Luoyang of the Wei Court was built at Luoyang.
237 AD	1st year, Jingchu, Mingdi of the Wei	The Garden of Fragrant Forest (Fang Lin Yuan) was completed and the Hill of Jingyang was piled up in Luoyang
The Jin Dynasty		
ca. 300 AD	ca. 1st year, Yongkang, Huidi	Shi Chong built a garden at the Golden Ravine in the northeastern outskirts of Luoyang, known as the Garden of Golden Ravine.
332 AD	7th year, Xianhe, Chengdi	The Palace of Jiankang was built in Jiankang (present-day Nanjing).
347 AD	3rd year, Yonghe, Mudi	An imperial garden called Hualin Garden was built at the southern bank of Xuanwu Lake in Jiankang. About a hundred years later, the Song of the Southern Dynasties built another garden called the Pleasure Garden to the east of Hualin Garden.
353~366 AD		Mogao Grottoes at Dunhuang, in present-day Gansu Province, were first dug out.
400 AD	4th year, Long'an, Andi	Buddhist Monk Huichi built the Temple of Samantabhadra (present-day the Wannian Temple) at Mount Emei in Sichuan.
413 AD	9th year, Yixi, Andi	Helianbobo built Tongwancheng, capital city of the Great Xia Dynasty (in presentday Inner Mongolia).
The Northern and Southern Dynasties		
452~464 AD	Wenchengdi, Northern Wei	Yungang Grottoes at Datong, Shanxi, were first hollowed out.
494~495 AD	18th~19th years, Taihe, Northern Wei	Longmen Grottoes at Luoyang, Henan, were first hollowed out.
513 AD	2nd year, Yanchang, Northern Wei	Grottoes of Bingling Temple, a Buddhist cave temple in Gansu, was built.
516 AD	1st year, Xiping, Northern Wei	Wooden Pagoda of the Temple of Everlasting Tranquillity (Yongning Temple) was erected up in Luoyang.
523 AD	4th year, Zhengguang, Northern Wei	Brick Pagoda of the Songyue Temple at Dengfeng in Henan was built.
The Sui Dynasty		
582	2nd year, Kaihuang, Wendi	Yuwen Kai was appointed to design and construct the capital city Daxing (present-day Xi'an), which was renamed as Chang'an in the Tang Dynasty.
586	6th year, Kaihuang, Wendi	Construction of the Longzang Buddhist Temple at Zhengding, Hebei, started. The temple was renamed as the Longxing Temple in the reign period of Emperor Kangxi of the Qing Dynasty.
595	15th year, Kaihuang, Wendi	Palace of Benevolence and Longevity (Ren Shou Gong) was built in Daxing, capital of the Sui Dynasty.
607	3rd year, Daye, Yangdi	One million men were sent to repair and restore the Great Wall.
611	7th year, Daye, Yangdi	The Four-Gate Pagoda, a single-storeyed pagoda, of Shentong Temple in Licheng, Shandong, was built.

Christian era	Chinese Dynastic Years	Events or Achievements
The Tang Dynasty		
618~916		Double-storeyed single-sealed dwelling houses came into being, while multi-storeyed buildings became on the wane.
627~648	Period of Zhenguan, Taizong	Mount Hua in Shaanxi, one of the Five Sacred Mountains in ancient China, was granted as the Golden Heavenly King, where the Temple of Western Sacred Mountain was built.
630	4th year, Zhenguan, Taizong	Orders were given to erect Confucian Temples in the schools of prefectures and counties all over the country.
636	10th year, Zhenguan, Taizong	Construction of Zhaoling Tomb (the Mausoleum of Emperor Taizong) began in Liquan County, Shaanxi.
651	2nd year, Yonghui,Gaozong	Taziks (the Arabian Empire) sent envoys to the Tang Court. Since then, the Islamic architecture came into being in China.
7th century		Huaisheng Si (literally, the Mosque in Memory of the Saint) was first built in Guangzhou, Guangdong.
652	3rd year, Yonghui,Gaozong	The Great Wild Goose Pagoda of Ci'en Temple in Chang'an (present-day Xi'an) was built.
669	2nd year, Zongzhang,	The Pagoda of Xuanzang was built in Xingjiao Temple in Chang'an.
681	1st year, Kaiyao, Gaozong	The Pagoda of Xiangji Temple in Chang'an was built.
683	1st year, Hongdao, Gaozong	Construction of Qianling Tomb (the Mausoleum of Emperor Gaozong) began in Qianxian County, Shaanxi.
707~709	1st~3rd years, Jinglong,Zhongzong	The Small Wild Goose Pagoda of Jianfu Temple in Chang'an was built.
714	2nd year, Kaiyuan,Xuanzong	Construction of Xingqing Palace in Chang'an started.
722	10th year, Kaiyuan, Xuanzong	The Tianchang Taoist Temple in Youzhou (present-day Beijing) was first built. The Temple was renamed as Baiyun Guan, or the Temple of White Clouds, in the early Ming Dynasty.
724	12th year, Kaiyuan, Xuanzong	Jianfu Palace at the foot of Qingcheng Mountain in Sichuan was first built.
725	13th year, Kaiyuan, Xuanzong	The Huaqing Pool with a detached palace was built at Lishan in Lintong County, Shaanxi. The Qujiang Pool with a recreation garden was built in Chang'an.
782	3rd year, Jianzhong, Dezong	The Main Hall of Nanchan Temple in Mount Wutai, Shanxi, was built.
857	11th year, Dazhong, Xuanzong	The Eastern Hall of Foguang Temple in Mount Wutai, Shanxi, was built.
The Five Dynasties		
956	3rd year, Xiande,Shizong, Late Zhou	The Later Zhou made Kaifeng the capital, and then, extended it on the basis of the capital of the Later Liang and Later Jin. Thereafter, Kaifeng was further developed especially when it was made capital of the Northern Song Dynasty.
959	6th year, Xiande,Shizong, Late Zhou	The Pagoda of Yunyan Temple at Suzhou, Jiangsu, was built.
The Northern Song and Liao (Khitan)Dynasties		
960~1279		Style and form of local dwelling houses were gradually finalized with less difference from those of the Qing period.
964	2nd year, Qiande,Taizu, the Song	The Temple of Central Sacred Mountain at Songshan, Henan, was renovated.
971	4th year, Kaibao,Taizu, the Song	The Pavilion of Buddha Fragrance (Foxiang Ge) at Longxing Temple in Zhengding, Hebei, was first built with a 24-metre-high bronze statue of Guanyin (Goddess of Mercy, or Avalokitesvara) housed in.
977	2nd year, Taipingxingguo,Taizong, the Song	The Longhua Pagoda was erected in Shanghai.
984	2nd year, Tonghe,Shengzong, the Liao	The Guanyin Pavilion and the Entrance Hall of Dule Temple at Jixian County in present day Tianjin were built.
996	14th year, Tonghe,Shengzong, the Liao	Libai Si of Niujie, or the Mosque of Ox Street, in Beijing was first built.
1009	2nd year, Dazhongxiangfu,Zhenzong, the Song	Tiankuang Dian (literally, the Hall of Godsend) of Dai Miao (Temple of Eastern Sacred Mountain) was built on the foot of Mount Tai, Shandong. Temple of Princess Aurora was built on the top of Mount Tai.
1009	2nd year, Dazhongxiangfu,Zhenzong, the Song	The Ashab Mosque at Quanzhou, Fujian, was first built.

Christian era	Chinese Dynastic Years	Events or Achievements
1038	7th year, Chongxi,Xingzong, the Liao	The Bhagavat Storage Hall (Bojia Jiaozang Dian) of the Lower Huayan Temple in Datong, Shanxi, was built.
1052	4th year, Huangyou,Renzong, the Song	The Hall of Sakyamuni (Moni Dian) of Longxing Temple in Zhengding, Hebei, was built.
1056	2nd year, Qingning,Daozong, the Liao	The Pagoda of Sakyamuni, or the Wooden Pagoda, of Fogong Temple at Yingxian, Shanxi, was erected.
1100	3rd year, Yuanfu,Zhezong, the Song	Li Jie finalized the book Building Standard, or treatise On Architectural Methods, which was promulgated by the Song Court in 1103 as building codes for design and construction works.
1102	1st year, Chongning,Huizong, the Song	The Shengmu Hall, or the Hall of Sacred Mother, of Jin Ci, a memorial temple of Jin, in Taiyuan, Shanxi, was restored.
1115	5th year, Zhenghe,Huizong, the Song	It is recorded that there were more than ten thousand workers everyday forced to build Mingtang for the emperor in Kaifeng.
1125	7th year, Xuanhe,Huizong, the Song	The Chuzu Nunnery, or the Hall of Patriarch, of Shaolin Temple in Dengfeng, Henan, was built.
12th century		The Minaret of Light was built in Huaisheng Si, or the Mosque in Memory of the Saint, in Guangzhou, Guangdong.

The Southern Song and Jin (Jurchen)Dynasties

Christian era	Chinese Dynastic Years	Events or Achievements
12th century		Han Tuozhou built his personal garden, called the Southern Garden, in Lin'an (present-day Hangzhou). Han Shizong built his personal garden, called Meigang Garden (literally, the Garden of Plum Blossom Ridge), in Lin'an.
1138	8th year, Shaoxing,Gaozong, the Song	The Song Court moved to Lin'an where the temporary palace was arranged. Lin'an was then decided upon as the temporary capital and was extended.
1150	2nd year, Tiande,Qingdi, the Jin	Wanyan Liang, emperor of the Jurchen (Jin), renamed Youzhou (present-day Beijing) as the Middle Capital of the Jurchen, and assigned Zhang Hao and Kong Yanzhou to the construction of the Middle Capital.
1163	3rd year, Dading,Shizong, the Jin	The Confucian Temple with its main hall, Dacheng Dian, at Pingyao, Shanxi, was built.
1240	12th year, Taizong of the Mongols	The Palace of Perpetual Happiness, or Yongle Gong, was built at Yongle Town in Yongji County, Shanxi. It is a Taoist temple in memory of Lu Dongbin, one of the Eight Taoist Immortals, and it was said that Yongle Town was Lu Dongbin's birthplace.
1267	4th year, Zhiyuan,Shizu of the Mongols	The Mongol Emperor Kublai Khan moved the capital to Youzhou (present-day Beijing), and renamed it as Dadu, or the Great Capital. Liu Bingzhong was appointed to plan and construct the Great Capital.
1269	6th year, ZhiyuanShizu of the Mongols	The Imperial College (the highest educational administration) was established in Dadu (the Great Capital).
1271	8th year, Zhiyuan,Shizu of the Yuan	In Miaoying Temple, a Lamasery in Beijing, the White Dagoba, which is a pagoda in Lamaist style, was erected. It is the earliest dagoba preserved intact in China.
1275	1st year, Deyou,Gongdi, the Song	Tomb of Puhading, sixteenth generation descendent of Mohammed, was built in Yangzhou, Jiangsu. Xianhe Si (literally, the Mosque of White Crane) was erected in Yangzhou.

The Yuan Dynasty

Christian era	Chinese Dynastic Years	Events or Achievements
13th century	Early Yuan Period	The Southern Temple of Saga in Saga County, Tibet, was built.
13th century	Early Yuan Period	The Hill of Longevity and the Imperial Lake were constructed in Dadu (the Great Capital) as the Imperial Garden of the Yuan Court. The Hill of Longevity was constructed on the Jade Flower Islet (or Qionghua Island) of the Jin, which is in Beihai Park of today's Beijing.
1302	6th year, Dade, Chengzong	The Confucian Temple in Dadu (present-day Beijing) was built.
1309	2nd year, Zhida, Wuzong	The Ashab Mosque at Quanzhou, Fujian, was renovated.
1323	3rd year, Zhizhi, Yingzong	Islamic Holy Tombs of Quanzhou, Fujian, were renovated.
1342	2nd year, Zhizheng, Shundi	Tian Ru, a Buddhist abbot, built the Shizi Lin (Garden of Lion Grove) in Suzhou.
1350	10th year, Zhizheng, Shundi	Huaisheng Si, or the Mosque in Memory of the Saint, in Guangzhou was renovated.
1356	16th year, Zhizheng, Shundi	The Mosque of Dongsi in Beijing was first built. It was renovated in 1447.
1363	23rd year, Zhizheng, Shundi	Mausoleum of Tuheluk Timur at Huocheng near Gulja (Yining), Xinjiang, was built.

The Ming Dynasty

Christian era	Chinese Dynastic Years	Events or Achievements
1368	1st year, Hongwu,Taizu	The Ming Court began to construct its imperial palace in Nanjing.

Christian era	Chinese Dynastic Years	Events or Achievements
1373	6th year, Hongwu, Taizu	Construction of the Capital City of Nanjing as well as the imperial palace was completed. General Xu Da was appointed to garrison the northern frontiers. Based on Hua Yunlong's proposal, the Great Wall was first rebuilt. It was renovated and extended several times in the Ming period. Temple for Offering Sacrifices to Emperors of the Past Dynasties was built on the southern slope of Qintian Hill in Nanjing.
1376~1383	9th~15th year, Hongwu, Tai	The Main Hall of Linggu Temple, a vaulted beamless building, in Nanjing was built.
1381	14th year, Hongwu, Taizu	Construction of Xiaoling Tomb (the Mausoleum of Emperor Taizu) started in Nanjing. The tomb was completed in 1405.
1407	5th year, Yongle, Chengzu	Construction of the Forbidden City in Beijing began.
1409	7th year, Yongle, Chengzu	Construction of Changling Tomb (the Mausoleum of Emperor Yongle) began in Changping County, Beijing.
1413	11th year, Yongle, Chengzu	An imperial order was given to build Taoist building complexes in Wudang Mountain, Hubei. It took 11 years to build up 8 palaces, 2 temples, 36 nunneries and 72 cliff temples.
1420	18th year, Yongle, Chengzu	City of Beijing with the Imperial City and Forbidden City included was completed. Capital of the Ming moved to Beijing. In Beijing, the Altar of Heaven, the Altar of Earth, the Imperial Ancestral Temple and the Altar of Agriculture were built.
1421	19th year, Yongle, Chengzu	The Three Great Halls of the Forbidden City were destroyed by fire. The Altar of Land and Grain in Beijing was built.
1436	1st year, Zhengtong, Yingzong	The Three Great Halls of the Forbidden City were rebuilt.
1442	7th year, Zhengtong,Yingzong	Libai Si of Niujie, or the Mosque of Ox Street, in Beijing was renovated. The Mosque was thoroughly restored and extended in 1696.
1444	9th year, Zhengtong,Yingzong	Zhihua Temple in Beijing was built.
1447	12th year, Zhengtong,Yingzong	Tashilunpo Monastery was built in Xigaze, Tibet.
1473	9th year, Chenghua,Xianzong	Diamond Throne Pagodas (Vajrasana Pagoda, which is a five-pagoda cluster) as well as the Temple of True Awakening where the Pagodas housed were built in Beijing.
1483~1487	19th~23rd year,Chenghua, Xianzong,	The layout of Confucian Temple in Qufu, Shandong, was completed in today's range and appearance.
1506~1521	Reign Period of Zhengde, Wuzong	Jichang Garden in Wuxi, Jiangsu, was built. It was famous for its "Eight-Scaled Ravine".
1509	4th year, Zhengde, Wuzong	Wang Xianchen, a censor of the Court, dismissed from office and returned to his home town Suzhou, where he built a garden and named it "Zhuozheng Yuan" (the Humble Administrator's Garden).
1519	14th year, Zhengde, Wuzong	The Palace of Heavenly Purity and Palace of Earthly Tranquillity in the Forbidden City of Beijing, were rebuilt.
1522~1566	Reign Period of Jiajing, Shizong	Liu Yuan, or the Lingering Garden, in Suzhou was first built. It was restored in the Qing Dynasty.
1530	9th year, Jiajing, Shizong	Altar of Earth, Altar of the Sun and Altar of the Moon were constructed in the outskirts of Beijing. A series of sacrifices to Heaven, Earth, the Sun and the Moon in the four outskirts of the capital city were restored. Altar of Agriculture was rebuilt.
1531	10th year, Jiajing, Shizong	Temple for Offering Sacrifices to Emperors of the Past Dynasties was built in Beijing.
1534	13th year, Jiajing, Shizong	The Altar of Heaven and Earth in Beijing was turned into the Altar of Heaven, or the Temple of Heaven.
1537	16th year, Jiajing, Shizong	The Hall of Mental Cultivation in the Forbidden City in Beijing was newly built.
1540	19th year, Jiajing, Shizong	The Stone Pailou of the Ming Tombs in Changping, Beijing, was erected.
1545	24th year, Jiajing, Shizong	The Imperial Ancestral Temple in Beijing was rebuilt. The Main Hall of the Temple of Heaven in Beijing was rebuilt. The hall which had been rectangular in plan was changed into a triple-eaved circular building, and renamed as the Hall of Prayer for Good Harvest.
1559	38th year, Jiajing, Shizong	Being a private garden in Shanghai, Yu Yuan was built by Pan Yunduan, a retired official. The rockery there was piled up by Zhang Nanyang, a famous rockery craftsman at that time.
1568	2nd year, Longqing, Muzong	General Qi Jiguang was appointed to garrison Jizhou near Beijing. Hence the Great Wall was restored and extended, and many more beacon towers and passes were built along the Great Wall.
1573~1619	Years of Wanli, Shenzong	Mi Wanzhong built his personal garden Shao Yuan in Beijing, which was famous for its four rarities: hill, water, flowers and rocks.

Christian era	Chinese Dynastic Years	Events or Achievements
1583	11th year, Wanli, Shenzong	Construction of Dingling Tomb (the Mausoleum of Emperor Wanli) in Changping, Beijing, started.
1583	26th year, Wanli, Shenzong	The Later Jin built Xingjingling Tombs (Tombs of Imperial Ancestors of the Qing) in Xinbin, Liaoning. The Tombs were renamed as Yongling Tombs in 1659.
1615	48th year, Wanli, Shenzong	The Three Great Halls of the Forbidden City in Beijing were rebuilt.
1629	2nd year, Chongzhen, Sizong	The Later Jin built Fuling Tomb (Tomb of Nurhachi, Emperor Taizu of the Qing) in Shenyang, Liaoning.
1634	7th year, Chongzhen, Sizong	Yuan ye, a treatise on Chinese gardens written by Ji Cheng, was published.
1640	13th year, Chongzhen, Sizong	The Qing Court built Dugong Hall (the Hall of Great Power) of the Imperial Palace in Shenyang.
1643	16th year, Chongzhen, Sizong	Zhaoling Tomb (Tomb of Huangtaiji, Emperor Taizong of the Qing) was first built in Shenyang, Liaoning.
The Qing Dynasty		
1645~1911		The traditional styles of local dwelling houses what we may catch sight of today had been formed to a great extent.
17th century	Early Qing Period	Tomb of Apak Hoja (Khwaja) in Kashi, Xinjiang, was first built. The tomb underwent several renovations in later years.
1644~1661	Reign Period of Shunzhi, Shizu	The West Imperial Garden (the Three Imperial Lakes with their surroundings) was reconstructed west of the Forbidden City in Beijing. The White Dagoba was erected on the top of the hill of the Jade Flower Islet in the Northern Lake (present-day Beihai Park).
1645	2nd year, Shunzhi, Shizu	Dalai Lama the Fifth rebuilt and extended the Potala Palace in Lhasa, Tibet.
1655	12th year, Shunzhi, Shizu	The Palace of Heavenly Purity and Palace of Earthly Tranquillity of the Forbidden City in Beijing were rebuilt.
1661	18th year, Shunzhi, Shizu	The Eastern Qing Tomb in Zunhua, Hebei, began to be constructed.
1662~1722	Reign Period of Kangxi, Shengzu	Chengqi Lou, a circular dwelling of the Hakkas was built in Yongding County, Fujian.
1663	2nd year, Kangxi, Shengzu	Xiaoling Tomb (the Mausoleum of Emperor Shunzhi) was completed in the Eastern Qing Tombs in Zunhua, Hebei.
1672	11th year, Kangxi, Shengzu	Temple of Marquis Wu Xiang in memory of Zhuge Liang was built in Chengdu, Sichuan.
1677	16th year, Kangxi, Shengzu	The layout of Dai Miao (the Temple of Eastern Sacred Mountain) in Mount Tai, Shandong, was completed in today's scale.
1680	19th year, Kangxi, Shengzu	Chengxin Yuan, an imperial garden at Jade Spring Hill in the western suburbs of Beijing, was built. It was renamed as Jingming Yuan, or the Garden of Light and Tranquillity, in later years.
1681	20th year, Kangxi, Shengzu	Jingling Tomb (the Mausoleum of Emperor Kangxi) started to be constructed in the Eastern Qing Tombs in Zunhua, Hebei.
1683	22nd year, Kangxi, Shengzu	Building complex of the Hall of Literary Glory in the Forbidden City in Beijing was rebuilt.
1684	23rd year, Kangxi, Shengzu	Changchun Yuan, or the Enjoying-the-Spring Garden, was constructed in the western suburbs of Beijing.
1689	28th year, Kangxi, Shengzu	Palace of Tranquil Longevity in the Forbidden City in Beijing was built.
1690	29th year, Kangxi, Shengzu	The Hall of Supreme Harmony in the Forbidden City began to be rebuilt. The hall was completed in 1695.
1703	42nd year, Kangxi, Shengzu	Construction of the Summer Resort at Chengde, Hebei, started.
1710	49th year, Kangxi, Shengzu	Guan Di Miao, or the Temple of Lord Guan was rebuilt in Guan's birthplace Xiexian County, Shanxi.
1718	57th year, Kangxi, Shengzu	Xiaodongling Tomb (the Tomb of Empress of Shunzhi) was built to the east of Xiaoling Tomb in the Eastern Qing Tombs in Zunhua, Hebei.
1725	3rd year, Yongzheng, Shizong	Construction of Yuanming Yuan, or the Garden of Perfect Splendor, or Garden of Perfection and Brightness, started in the northwestern suburbs of Beijing. It was then extended and developed to 40 scenic spots during the period of Emperor Qianlong.
1730	8th year, Yongzheng, Shizong	Tailing Tomb (the Mausoleum of Emperor Yongzheng) was first built in Yizhou (present-day Yixian, Hebei). The Tomb was completed in 1737.
1734	12th year, Yongzheng, Shizong	The Board of Works promulgated Gongcheng Zuofa Zeli, or the Structural Regulations, as building codes for design and construction works.
1735	13th year, Yongzheng, Shizong	Fragrant Hill Summer Resort for the emperor was built in the Western Hills of Beijing.
1736~1796	Reign period of Qianlong, Gaozong	Ge Yuliang, a well-known rockery craftsman, built the Huanxiu Shanzhuang (the Nestling-in-Green Mountain Villa) in Suzhou.

Christian era	Chinese Dynastic Years	Events or Achievements
1745	10th year, Qianlong, Gaozong	Fragrant Hill Summer Resort in the western hills of Beijing was extended and renamed as Jingyi Yuan (the Garden of Congenial Tranquillity).
1746~1748	11th~13th years, Qianlong, Gaozong	The Central Palatial Complex of the Imperial Palace in Shenyang was extended. Two lodges, or building compounds, were built and added to the east and west of the Central Complex.
1750	15th year, Qianlong, Gaozong	The Pavilion of the Rain of Flowers was erected in the Forbidden City in Beijing. Construction of Qingyi Yuan, or the Garden of Clear Ripples, started. It was an imperial garden including the Hill of Longevity and the Kunming Lake in the western suburbs of Beijing. It took 14 years to complete this garden.
1751	16th year, Qianlong, Gaozong	Changchun Yuan (the Garden of Eternal Spring) and Qichun Yuan (the Garden of Blossoming Spring) were built to the east of Yuanming Yuan (the Garden of Perfect Splendor).
1752	17th year, Qianlong, Gaozong	Roofing tiles of the Hall of Prayer for Good Harvest in the Temple of Heaven, Beijing, were rebuilt with blue glazed tiles. The Imperial Palace in Shenyang was renovated.
1755	20th year, Qianlong, Gaozong	Puning Si (Temple of Universal Tranquillity), in Chengde, Hebei, was built. Its main hall, Dacheng Ge (Pavilion of Mahayana) was built to imitate the main hall of Sangye Temple in Tibet.
1764	29th year, Qianlong, Gaozong	Anyuan Miao Temple in Chengde, Hebei, was Built.
1765	30th year, Qianlong, Gaozong	Song Zongyuan, a retired official, built Wangshi Yuan, or the Garden of the Master of Fishing Nets, in Suzhou.
1766	31st year, Qianlong,	Pule Si Temple in Chengde, Hebei, was built.
1767~1771	32nd~36th years, Qianlong, Gaozong	Temple of the Potaraka Doctrine (Putuo Zongcheng Zhi Miao) in Chengde, Hebei, was built.
1774	39th year, Qianlong, Gaozong	Wenyuan Ge Library in the Forbidden City, Beijing, was built.
1778	43rd year, Qianlong, Gaozong	The Western Palatial Complex of the Imperial Palace in Shenyang was built. The Mosque with Su Gong Tower in Turpan, Xinjiang, was completed.
1779~1780	44th~45th years, Qianlong, Gaozong	Temple of Sumeru Happiness and Longevity (Xu Mi Fu Shou Zhi Miao) in Chengde, Hebei, was built.
1781	46th year, Qianlong, Gaozong	Wensu Ge Library, Yangxi Zhai Study and Jiayin Tang Hall of the Imperial Palace in Shenyang were built.
1783	48th year, Qianlong, Gaozong	Biyong, or the Main Hall of the Imperial College (Guo Zi Jian), in Beijing was built.
1784	49th year, Qianlong, Gaozong	Dagobas of the City of Complete Purification (Qing Jing Hua Cheng Ta) of the West Yellow Temple in Beijing were erected.
18th century		Taer Temple in Huangzhong, Qinghai, was built.
1796	1st year, Jiaqing, Renzong	Changling Tomb (the Mausoleum of Emperor Jiaqing) of t h e Western Qing Tombs in Yixian, Hebei, was first built. It was completed eight years later.
1804	9th year, Jiaqing, Renzong	Three Palatial Complexes with Lodges of the Central Complex of the Imperial Palace in Shenyang were renovated.
1832	12th year, Daoguang, Renzong	Muling Tomb (the Mausoleum of Emperor Daoguang) of the Western Qing Tombs in Yixian, Hebei, was first built. It was completed four years later.
1859	9th year, Xianfeng, Wenzong	Dingling Tomb (the Mausoleum of Emperor Xianfeng) of the Eastern Qing Tombs in Zunhua, Hebei, was first built.
1860	10th year, Xianfeng, Wenzong	Yuanming Yuan (the Garden of Perfect Splendor) and Qingyi Yuan (the Garden of Clear Ripples) were destroyed and burnt down by the Anglo-French Allied forces.
1873	12th year, Tongzhi, Muzong	Dingdongling Tombs (Tombs of Empress Dowagers Cixi and Ci'an) were first built in the Eastern Qing Tombs in Zunhua, Hebei. The Tombs were completed in 1879.
1875	1st year, Guangxu, Dezong	Huiling Tomb (the Mausoleum of Emperor Tongzhi) of the Eastern Qing Tombs in Zunhua, Hebei, was built.
1888	14th year, Guangxu, Dezong	Qingyi Yuan was rebuilt and renamed as Yihe Yuan (the Summer Palace) under Empress Dowager Cixi. Jianfu Palace of Qingcheng Mountain, Sichuan, was rebuilt.
1909	1st year, Xuantong	Chongling Tomb (the Mausoleum of Emperor Guangxu) was built in the Western Qing Tombs in Yixian, Hebei.

The Excellence of Ancient Chinese Architecture, Chinese Edition
Author: Wei Ran
Chief Planner: Zhou Yi
Editorial Members: Wang Boyang, Wei Ran, Wang Xuelin
Editor in Charge: Wang Boyang, Ma Yan
Photographers: Zhang Zhenguang, Wei Ran, Chen Xiaoli, Li Dongxi, Cao Yang

The Excellence of Ancient Chinese Architecture, English Edition
Chief Planner: Zhang Huizhen
Translators: Pan Jingyi, San Mu
Editor in Charge: Qi Linlin, Zhang Huizhen
Photographers: Zhang Zhenguang, Wei Ran, Chen Xiaoli, Li Dongxi, Cao Yang
Cover Design: Fu Jinhong
Layout Design: Xiao Jinxing

The Excellence of
Ancient Chinese Architecture

Buddhist Buildings 佛教建筑
Buddhist Monasteries, Pagodas and Stone Caves

Wei Ran

© 2012 China Architecture & Building Press
Published and Distributed by China Architecture & Building Press
ISBN 978-7-112-14288-0 (22343)
CIP data available on request
www.cabp.com.cn

Printed on acid-free and chlorine-free bleached paper

Printed in China